About This Book

Why is this topic important?

The return on investment for coaching is multiple times the initial investment, and the payoffs are tangible: sustained superior performance and commitment to self, organizations, and goals. The more coaching happens, the more high per-forming individuals and teams become. Coaching is an investment in people that leads to bottom-line results!

What can you achieve with this book?

Coaching for Commitment has something to offer to everyone. The manager who is looking to foster independence and innovation, the executive who wants to hone strategic and interpersonal skills, the HR professional who wants to effec-tively develop talent, the teacher who is trying to communicate differently with students and team members, the employee who is stuck in a rut and is looking for growth and opportunity, the parent who is looking for a new and creative way to interact with the kids, or the coaching professional who is looking for a new way of re-energizing his or her coaching. This book is for the new and the novice coach, as well as for the seasoned and savvy.

How is this book organized?

This book contains nine chapters and five appendices. From commitment to coaching and back to commitment, it is loaded with tools, examples, and sample coaching conversations that illuminate the use of the coaching process, model, and skills.

About Pfeiffer

Pfeiffer serves the professional development and hands-on resource needs of training and human resource practitioners and gives them products to do their jobs better. We deliver proven ideas and solutions from experts in HR development and HR management, and we offer effective and customizable tools to improve workplace performance. From novice to seasoned professional, Pfeiffer is the source you can trust to make yourself and your organization more successful.

Essential Knowledge Pfeiffer produces insightful, practical, and comprehensive materials on topics that matter the most to training and HR professionals. Our Essential Knowledge resources translate the expertise of seasoned professionals into practical, how-to guidance on critical workplace issues and problems. These resources are supported by case studies, worksheets, and job aids and are frequently supplemented with CD-ROMs, websites, and other means of making the content easier to read, understand, and use.

Essential Tools Pfeiffer's Essential Tools resources save time and expense by offering proven, ready-to-use materials—including exercises, activities, games, instruments, and assessments—for use during a training or team-learning event. These resources are frequently offered in looseleaf or CD-ROM format to facilitate copying and customization of the material.

Pfeiffer also recognizes the remarkable power of new technologies in expanding the reach and effectiveness of training. While e-hype has often created whizbang solutions in search of a problem, we are dedicated to bringing convenience and enhancements to proven training solutions. All our e-tools comply with rigorous functionality standards. The most appropriate technology wrapped around essential content yields the perfect solution for today's on-the-go trainers and human resource professionals.

www.pfeiffer.com

Essential resources for training and HR professionals

This book is dedicated to Tammy Zehnder,
our special angel, whose celestial presence
continues to make it possible for us
to finish projects like these,
while still finding time to dance in the rain,
play in the snow, and celebrate that life is good!

Pfeiffer™

Coaching for Commitment

ACHIEVING SUPERIOR PERFORMANCE FROM INDIVIDUALS AND TEAMS

THIRD EDITION

Cindy Coe

Amy Zehnder

Dennis Kinlaw

John Wiley & Sons, Inc.

Published by Pfeiffer
An Imprint of Wiley
989 Market Street, San Francisco, CA 94103-1741
www.pfeiffer.com

For additional copies/bulk purchases of this book in the U.S. please contact 800-274-4434.

Pfeiffer books and products are available through most bookstores. To contact Pfeiffer directly call our Customer Care Department within the U.S. at 800-274-4434, outside the U.S. at 317-572-3985, fax 317-572-4002, or visit www.pfeiffer.com.

Pfeiffer also publishes its books in a variety of electronic formats. Some content that appears in print may not be available in electronic books.

Library of Congress Cataloging-in-Publication Data

Coe, Cindy.
   Coaching for commitment : achieving superior performance from individuals and teams / Cindy Coe, Amy Zehnder, and Dennis Kinlaw.— 3rd ed.
     p.   cm.
   Rev. ed. of: Coaching for commitment / Dennis Kinlaw. 2nd ed. c1999.
   Includes bibliographical references and index.
   ISBN-13: 978-0-7879-8249-2 (cloth)
    1. Personnel management.   2. Employees—Coaching of.   3. Employees—Training of.
4. Employee motivation. I. Zehnder, Amy, 1966- II. Kinlaw, Dennis C. III. Kinlaw, Dennis C. Coaching for commitment. IV. Title.
HF5549.K498 2008
658.3'124—dc22

                                              2007033231

Acquiring Editor: Martin Delahoussaye
Director of Development: Kathleen Dolan Davies
Developmental Editor: Susan Rachmeler
Production Editor: Dawn Kilgore
Editor: Rebecca Taff
Editorial Assistant: Julie Rodriquez
Manufacturing Supervisor: Becky Morgan
Printed in the United States of America

Printing   10 9 8 7 6 5 4 3 2

CONTENTS

ACKNOWLEDGMENTS

"It's wonderful to be blessed with more friends than time!"

—CC

FIRST AND FOREMOST, this edition of *Coaching for Commitment* would not have been possible without the foundational work that was provided by the late Dennis C. Kinlaw.

This book is dedicated to all of the people who make our lives rich and full, who help us to know we are blessed and to those who make it possible for us to do what we love every day! It is because of you that we dedicated ourselves, and a few years, to this incredible project! We hope you may find just a little of the passion we feel when we experience the impact of coaching.

We would like to thank all of the coaching mentors we have had who provided us with the knowledge, skills, practice, and feedback to make us the coaches we are today. Thanks also go to all of the people whom we have coached and whom we continue to learn from, as well as those who have provided us with the insight and wisdom necessary to take on this endeavor.

Thanks to Deborah Gay, Ph.D., for introducing us to the world of coaching as a career and profession and for being a mentor, dear friend, and our biggest cheerleader. More thanks go out to Pat White, Master Certified Coach (MCC) and CEO of The Spectrum Group, for working with Amy so that she could achieve her Professional Certified Coach (PCC) designation through the International Coach Federation (ICF) and also for being part of the round one peer review before our final draft was even complete and cohesive! Your feedback was very valuable in our rewrites (of which there were many)!

Thank you also to our round one peer reviewers: Alison House, O.D. (House Vision Center, Pueblo, CO), whose supportive comments and critical eye were so helpful for us to see things from the perspective of someone new to coaching, and James Gunn (Supervisor, Clinical Pastoral Education, Penrose-St. Francis Health Services, Colorado Springs, CO), who provided us some incredible feedback delivered with the utmost finesse and humor! You are all on our "we owe you one" list! Thank you also goes to our round two final draft reviewers!

A special thank you to our editor, Martin Delahoussaye of Pfeiffer, for his interest in this revision and his belief that we were the right people to make this merger of the minds, thoughts, and ideas possible. Our gratitude goes also to Julie Rodriguez, editorial assistant, who made great things happen before our round two pilot coaching workshop!

Bill Coscarelli—Professor Extraordinaire! You magically appeared in our lives just when we needed some statistical analysis performed on the CSI (Coaching Skills Inventory). Talk about timing! You are amazing! Thank you so much for your contributions on this project and we wish you much success in your own endeavors!

Thank you to the International Coach Federation for putting structure and guidance around the growing world of coaching.

We would like to thank Heidi Onsted for introducing us to Beth Hobbs, who welcomed us into Gillette Children's Specialty Healthcare (St. Paul, MN) and allowed us to use a large group of managers as a "test pilot" group to perfect the two-day Coaching for Commitment workshop! You have no idea how much those two days meant to this entire project! It is you and the wonderful pilot group we have to thank for the final rewrite that brought all the pieces of this package together! Thank you for your participation and insights!

Additional thanks go to the colleagues who have supported our efforts, sent words and tokens of encouragement, and understood our "spread thin" existence over the course of this project: Theresa, Jeanie, Mike, Jeff, Lyle, Kao, Rose x 3, Terri, Kristin, George, Kristi,

Anna, D'Andrea, Janet, Patsy, Nina, Sylvia, Paula, Matthew, Laura, Paul, Mark, Kathy, Debbie, Sue, Jane, Lorna, Karen, Laurie, Patrick, Marshall, Kristy, and Sara. Your patience and understanding were so appreciated!

Thank you to the dedicated group of early childhood education professionals from Cleveland, Ohio, who have reinforced our faith in the education system and the people who work in it. Your input provided the fine-tuning we needed to perfect the end product you see today. Bliss to you!

Thank you also to the Pikes Peak Metropolitan Community Church board of directors for your faithful prayers, comic relief, and for providing us a periodic distraction by way of facilitating your team-building workshops! Bless you!

And finally, we would like to thank all of our wonderful neighbors, friends, and family for encouraging us, cheering us on, knowing when to drag us out of the house, when to leave us alone, when to check in on us, when to feed us, and when to run interference! For those of you who visited at your own risk during this process, we apologize, for we were certainly not 100 percent present and accounted for . . . There's always next year! For those who managed to get us out of ourselves, if only for an hour or a weekend, and those who tempted and cajoled and kept on trying, we thank you as well. Most of all, we thank you for your constant encouragement and for cheering us on even in the final few months when the book took on a life of its own and consumed us. Your support and tolerance (even when you didn't hear from us for months on end) was incredible! Thanks to Floreen, Elwin, Tom, Ora, Heidi, Bruce, Wendy, Gary W., Gwen, Skip, Cindy, Larry, Martha, Bill, Karen, Doug, Gina, Tanner, Jordan, Mary Ann, Alan, Brandon, Shelly, Gary M., Alison, Vince, Lorraine, Bettina, Kevin, Forrestine, Rachael, Jason, Dawn, John, Fiona, Rob, Sophie, Hans, Sally, Lynn, Hector, Bob, Jeanette, Michelle, Chris, Donyelle, Shirley, Casey, Samir, Nerma, Mary, Cort, and anyone else we may have inadvertently overlooked (our sincere apologies). We can come out and play now!

One more very special thank you goes to guitar teacher Paul Parker for understanding why Amy had no brain cells left to practice her guitar during this project and who graciously agreed to postpone many lessons. Paul, I'm ready again!

Cheers and Mahalo!

CC & Doc

Authors' Disclaimer: In order to protect the confidentiality of our *real* clients and workshop participants, you may notice your name used in a scenario or example in this book or in the companion workshop. This usage was intended as a compliment to you and does not necessarily reflect your actual attitudes, thoughts, comments or behaviors. You are simply an actor playing a role! Lights, Camera, Action . . . !

*"This is one of the most complete coaching skills documents
I have ever read. It is written to instruct both the line manager
who wants to pick up coaching skills as well as the person
wanting to coach outside of the on-the-job setting."*

Pat White, MCC

Target Audience

This book was written with various readers in mind, including coaching professionals, executives, employees, HR professionals, small business owners, administrators, teachers, doctors, dentists, lawyers, parents, college students, aspiring professionals, and pretty much anyone who interacts with people.

Coaching is for anyone who has a desire to help others find their own answers and achieve goals by committing to action. "Coaching is not just a function; it is a state of mind."

This book is a practical, "how to" guide to coaching for everyone and for all kinds of coaching. Whether you are coaching face-to-face, on the fly (coaching moment), by phone, email, or managing a virtual team, this book is for you!

This book is written for you: the new, old, skilled, novice, or aspiring coach, and it is designed to teach you effective coaching strategies and techniques that will assist you on your journey to becoming a skillful coach!

How Can Coaching for Commitment Help You?

Leaders, you will find in this book a philosophy of coaching, tools and skills that can become the foundation for any initiative to make coaching part of managing by objective (MBOs), an operating function for everyone from executive to employee, and ultimately, part of the culture in your organization.

Human resource (HR) professionals, directors, managers, and consultants alike, who have responsibility for developing, delivering, or implementing programs on coaching, this book will not only provide the tools to improve your own coaching skills but it is also the conceptual basis needed to conduct coaching workshops (especially with the corresponding Coaching for Commitment Workshop materials). The concepts within this book are instrumental for developing talent.

Coaching professionals or executive coaches, for some time now a demand for trained coaching professionals has been growing. Organizations are hiring these professionals to coach executives and other leaders, to help them understand various aspects of their own performance, gain clarity about the way they conduct personal interactions, understand the way they solve problems, and help them clarify their own career and performance goals. HR professionals who intend to function as professional coaches will find information and ideas that will better equip them to perform this function.

Small-to medium-sized business owners, other professionals or aspiring professionals, and anyone else who coaches people (such as employees, team leaders, parents, teachers, and administrators), there are tools in this book for you as well. The coaching skills, model, and techniques can be applied to almost anyone: students, peers, co-workers, patients, staff, family members, and friends.

Third Edition Enhancements

In the very first edition of *Coaching for Commitment: Managerial Strategies for Obtaining Superior Performance*, authored by Dennis Kinlaw and published in 1989, the primary need at the time was to help managers and supervisors recognize coaching as one of their most important functions and to give them a tool to become successful coaches. In 1999, when the second edition of *Coaching for Commitment* was published, the focus had shifted to an employee-centric viewpoint wherein empowered employees were expected to operate as leaders, thus shifting the focus of coaching to include every member of an organization to act as a coach to others.

This third edition of *Coaching for Commitment: Achieving Superior Performance from Individuals and Teams* takes all of the foundational work of coaching that was created by Dennis Kinlaw and expands it into a pure coaching approach, as defined by the latest coaching strategies and methodologies. Since 1999, coaching has not only become highly popular as a leadership practice, but has become a highly sought after profession. As the world of coaching grew, so did its regulatory counterparts. Now, coaching is professionalized by organizations such as the International Coach Federation (www.coachfederation.org). Accredited coaching schools have emerged to teach coaching skills and to provide insight on effective coaching practices and strategies. *Coaching for Commitment: Achieving Superior Performance from Individuals and Teams* has been enhanced to include new coaching competencies, methodologies, and successful strategies that will assist you in becoming a skillful coach. It provides information on the latest definitions of what coaching is and ways to be successful as a coach.

Furthermore, and with all due respect to Dennis Kinlaw, who has since passed away, two new authors are introduced with this revision: Cindy Coe and Amy Zehnder. The majority of concepts in this edition had their genesis in Kinlaw's original work. Our goal as the new authors was to keep the merger of authors relatively seamless to the reader and to keep Kinlaw's Coaching for Commitment legacy alive.

To accomplish this goal, all of the material from the second edition was thoroughly revised into a more logical sequence with more visual representation and fully updated to reflect current coaching trends. Many of the original concepts from the second edition are embedded throughout this edition with significant enhancements.

Occasionally, specific examples, quotes, or experiences are highlighted as Kinlaw's work, and hence he will be referred to in the third person.

- Dennis Kinlaw made the tie between coaching and commitment more obvious in his second edition; this edition takes it one step further and makes commitment a part of the coaching model. This reaffirms that coaching is a powerful strategy for strengthening the commitment of people to do their level best at all times.

- One major modification is how the *person being coached* is referred to. There has always been confusion in this area, and historically there have been many names for the person being coached (client, coachee, team member, etc.). For this book, its companion assessment and training workshop, the person(s) being coached, whether it is a single person or multiple people, will be called the **PBC**. In most cases throughout the text, "person being coached (PBC)" will be used for the *first use only* in each chapter with the PBC acronym being used for the remainder of the chapter. In some cases the plural acronym "PBCs" will be used. "You," on the other hand, is used to make reference to *your role as the coach*. Thus, when certain components and skills are addressed to *you*, we are referring to *you, as the coach*.

- In Chapter 1, the Coaching for Commitment philosophy was brought up-to-date and made more relevant for the times and today's world of business, leadership, and coaching.

- Kinlaw introduced *counseling, mentoring, confronting and challenging, and tutoring* as types of coaching in the second edition. In Chapter 2, this edition is distinctly different from others in its use of roles versus types or styles of coaching. Here, there is only one role where coaching occurs, which is called the *coach role*. If you are not coaching, you are in a different role. The *coach role* is introduced to better differentiate between various other roles that people play in the workplace. The new roles reflect more relevant terms being used by and recognized in the corporate and regulatory world today. A *role model* graphic delineates these roles of *manager, instructor, mentor, and coach*. Your tendencies to gravitate to each role are measured with the new CSI (Coaching Skills Inventory) and represented visually using the *role model* graphic.

The *manager* role is new to this edition, as people have recently begun to question how their roles as managers differ from the *coach role*. Therefore, this edition clearly differentiates between the two roles.

Kinlaw's *tutoring* was changed to the *instructor* role. The term *instructor* is more accurate in describing the nature of this role and is also more relevant to today's business climate.

Kinlaw's *mentoring* is retained as a role and will hereafter be referred to as the *mentor* role.

Kinlaw's former *confronting* and *challenging* are recognized most commonly in organizations as "performance coaching conversations." Today, the word *confronting* (or confrontation), when used in organizations, carries a very negative connotation, and the word *challenging* in the coaching world is more in line with making requests that stretch people beyond normal limits—which is *sometimes* appropriate in the performance improvement conversation and *is also applicable to all other coaching conversations*. Because of this, confronting and challenging is no longer used as a type of coaching or a role. There is, however, a section on Performance Coaching in Chapter 7, and the techniques identified by Kinlaw have been incorporated in the new CLEAR coaching skills.

Finally, counseling can no longer be called a type of coaching due to recent regulatory controversy. Over the past few years, the process of making distinctions for what coaching is and is not has become a matter of great discussion. Many of us in the coaching profession contend that our role is clearly set apart from other vocations such as consulting, counseling, and psychotherapy. The coaching industry as a whole is also very clear that coaching is not therapy. However, the topics of counseling and therapy have received a lot of attention from coaching schools and coaching governing boards, as well as psychological governing boards, in recent years. Because of this scrutiny and controversy in distinguishing coaching from therapy and counseling, this edition does not use Kinlaw's counseling, thus eliminating any close ties to the therapeutic world because coaching *is not* therapy. This topic is discussed in greater detail in Chapter 2.

- In Chapter 3, the biggest addition to this book comes in the form of a visual representation of the entire coaching process, which is now inclusive of a coaching model and skills. A Coaching Prism visual was created to illustrate how all of the coaching components come together to create successful coaching conversations; included in the chapter are the elements of trust, the InDiCom coaching model, and CLEAR coaching skills. Trust is more than a skill. It is considered the key component of all successful coaching conversations and essential throughout all stages of the coaching model. Because of this, it has been given a chapter of its own (Chapter 4) and is no longer recognized as one of Kinlaw's general skills, formerly referred to as Indicating Respect.

- In Chapter 5, Kinlaw's two coaching processes (Responding to Needs and Initiating Alternatives) were merged into *one coaching model* called InDiCom. Between the first and second editions, Kinlaw simplified his two models; moving to one model in this third edition simplifies things even further. The reason for this modification is that all of Kinlaw's types of coaching from the second edition—counseling, mentoring, confronting, and tutoring—employ the same core skills and move through the same coaching process. They differ only in the initial approach.

The new InDiCom Coaching Model consists of three stages: Involve, Discover, and Commit.

- Chapter 6 debuts the new CLEAR coaching skills, which can be used in all stages of the InDiCom coaching model. Kinlaw's general coaching skills were redefined, combined, and turned into the coaching skills acronym—CLEAR.

- Plan to Coach, Chapter 7, details how to plan for and conduct performance coaching conversations and provides an in-depth discussion of the various coaching channels (face-to-face and virtual) that can be used to conduct your coaching conversations.

- Chapter 8 is devoted to all new, extended coaching conversation samples. These examples support the Coaching Prism, InDiCom coaching model, and CLEAR coaching skills. There are also two coaching moment examples as well as one email coaching example. These examples demonstrate that coaching can occur using just about any means and that it is a function for everyone—not just appointed leaders in organizations!

- In Chapter 9, Creating a Coaching for Commitment Culture, the scope of coaching remains consistent in that coaching is seen as a function that can and should be performed by all persons at all levels in all organizations, rather than just a function for managers, supervisors, and other leaders. This new Creating a Coaching for Commitment Culture chapter focuses on how anyone can create a coaching culture that is reciprocal in nature and extensible to the entire organization—even if it starts with one team. This is based on the premise that superior teams are characterized by leaders who are perceived and valued as good coaches and that, in instances in which team development and team performance have fulfilled expectations, you can expect to find team leaders and employees spending a good bit of their time coaching one another and coaching their teams. For this to occur, first the leader must create the conditions that foster a coaching for commitment culture, which includes educating and providing resources (such as this book or the *Coaching for Commitment Discussion Guide*) to team members about coaching and its components, as well as modeling the way. Even if you are not in a position to influence your entire organization or its leaders, you can commit to Creating a Coaching for Commitment Culture for those within your scope of influence. A new guide was created and included in this chapter to help you create a Coaching for Commitment action plan.

Additional Coaching for Commitment Components

In addition to revising this book, revisions were also made to other components of the package. Each of these items can be purchased through Pfeiffer (www.pfeiffer.com). Some can be purchased as a package.

Two-Day Coach Training Workshop

The workshop contains a fully revised, interactive, experiential, and comprehensive two-day training program on the Coaching for Commitment content with extensions to apply it to the real world of business and coaching. The workshop components are:

- Facilitator's Guide
- Participant Workbook
- DVD/video of coaching samples
- CD-ROM, which contains a slide presentation and supplemental materials
- Coaching Skills Inventory: Self

- Coaching Skills Inventory: Observer
- Discussion Guide

The last three items are described in more detail next.

Coaching Skills Inventory (CSI)

The Coaching Skills Inventory (CSI) contains three components:

- CSI: Self-Assessment
- CSI: Observer Assessment
- CSI Administrator's Guide

The *CSI: Self* has been changed to identify (1) a coaching gap compared to an ideal, (2) the role(s) you gravitate toward, and (3) proficiency levels in using certain coaching skills during interactions with others. We recommend taking the assessment before you read this book. It will provide you with a great starting point for your reading.

The CSI also has a 360-degree feedback component. Use the *CSI: Observer* to get a holistic view of the behaviors and actions you exhibit. For a full 360-degree view, obtain an observer assessment from your boss, three direct reports (if applicable), and three others. Depending on the nature of your work and/or your purpose in using this inventory, "others" may include peers, partners, vendors, customers, or students. The *CSI: Observer* also makes a great follow-up assessment to check your progress.

The *CSI Administrator's Guide* is designed to assist anyone who is administering the CSI as part of the Coaching for Commitment workshop, as part of another leadership or coaching program, or as a stand-alone assessment. Thus, this Guide is sold separately from the workshop package.

Coaching for Commitment Discussion Guide

Are you planning to create a Coaching for Commitment culture or simply help others to understand what Coaching for Commitment and/or what this book is all about? This helpful booklet was designed for you to share the basics of Coaching for Commitment with others. Using the guide will assist you in providing others with a foundation for understanding what you are trying to do when in the coach role. It will help you generate a spirit of commitment to coaching with your team or organization. And it also makes a great refresher tool for you.

Introduction

"In today's workplace, everyone can be a coach."
—Dennis C. Kinlaw, Ed. D.

SUSTAINED SUPERIOR performance occurs, most of all, because people are committed to do their level best all of the time. Coaching is a proven strategy for building such commitment.

This book is about coaching and is based on a combined total of over forty years of coaching experience, researching and writing about coaching, and teaching the value and skills of coaching to others. It describes coaching as a strategy for improving performance that has special utility in today's climate of intense competitiveness for total customer satisfaction, continuous improvement, and the drive to deliver products and services 100 percent perfect 100 percent of the time. It also describes coaching as a function of helping people discover new and creative solutions to complex and difficult situations, while becoming more committed to taking action.

We can change organizational systems, work processes, technology, and structures. We can re-organize, re-engineer, and re-invent organizations. We can advocate stewardship for leaders, tough-mindedness for leaders, or high-mindedness for leaders. We can involve people and empower them. We can use a wide range of alternatives to improve performance. But, unless we create the commitment of people who apply these alternatives to do their very best all of the time, no change in culture, systems, or leadership will work. If conducted properly, coaching is one proven strategy for creating such commitment.

Coaching is a way to develop people so they can achieve superior performance and commitment to sustained growth and positive relationships. It is the process of helping people discover creative solutions to complex situations. Coaching provides a safe environment for identifying opportunities and making them a reality. Coaching is based on the philosophy that people have the insight, experience, and knowledge to draw from in order to make decisions and move forward toward their ideal.

Coaching is too closely tied to the improvement of performance to imagine that it can ever become dated. It has been of value for equipping people to perform and gaining their commitment to perform well for as long as people have assisted one another to do their best.

Coaching works at *every level* and in *all* organizational relationships. It works to improve the performance of individuals (from employee to executive), it works to improve the performance of teams, and ultimately, it works to improve the performance of entire organizations. It works because it creates the major factors that lead to commitment, it clarifies goals and priorities, it helps people understand what is important and what is not, it invites people to demonstrate competent influence over their performance and careers, it helps people to resolve performance problems, it challenges people, it improves the knowledge and skills that people need to do their best, and it conveys to others just how important and appreciated they are.

Commitments that are a result of coaching are powerful because they are a result of buy-in and a personal investment. Oftentimes these commitments are tied to personal values and an internal desire to change or improve.

The Changing Coach Role

Coaching has always been an important managerial and supervisory function, but today coaching is everyone's job. The primary reason for the increased importance and wider application of coaching is not only because traditional jobs of leadership have changed, but because the *coach role* has evolved over the past few years into a role of its own. Coaching is now rarely concentrated solely in the jobs of manager and supervisor. Coaching has become a function that is exercised by many people in a variety of vocations and capacities.

"Formal" leaders, under whatever name, be it executive, manager,-supervisor, or team leader, are responsible for producing results. They are responsible to achieve production quotas, develop new products, meet sales goals, increase revenues, ensure technical excellence, solve problems in complex systems, and complete an almost endless variety of projects within a limited amount of time. Most of all, they are responsible that customers are totally satisfied with the products and services they deliver.

What has become transparently obvious is that leaders may sometimes contribute directly to results through their technical competence or interpersonal skills, but *most* of their results are achieved indirectly through the knowledge, skills, and commitment of others. Thus, requiring leaders to be more conscious of and effective at talent management and succession planning.

At one time leaders were encouraged to believe that they could achieve results through people by controlling the performance of others. They were encouraged to believe that if they could write enough policies, make enough rules, invoke enough rewards and punishments, solve everything for everyone, practice rigorous oversight, and critically appraise performance, they just might plan, organize, and direct people up to a level of satisfactory performance.

These days, no one *really* believes that satisfactory performance is good enough. Satisfactory performance is built on the notions of "average" and "reasonable limits." In the now and forever world of immediacy and increasing national and global competition, if leaders accept the goal of satisfactory performance, they inevitably accept a loss in competitiveness, a decline in market share, stagnant capital growth, and decreased profitability.

One leadership lesson that most organizations have apparently begun to learn is that people may do *satisfactory* work because they are forced to do so by a variety of controls, but they will only do *superior* work because they want to—that is, because they are personally committed to doing so. The traditional control model of leadership does not work, and here are some of the reasons why:

- People can, perhaps, be managed and supervised to a satisfactory level of performance—provided there are enough controls, work is predictable, and managers or supervisors have time to give continual and direct oversight. Rarely do these conditions exists today. Thus, performance more and more comes under the control of the individual.

- People have value because they can respond to unplanned events, provide an individualized approach, and take advantage of unexpected opportunities. People in organizations have value over technology and systems because they take care of hundreds of problems and respond to hundreds of opportunities that no one knew would occur. Superior performance is clearly a function of such behavior.

- People have an enormous amount of control over what they do and how much effort they put into their jobs. The majority of people in the majority of jobs could do a good deal more or a good deal less, and nobody would be the wiser—especially their immediate supervisors.

- The only way for leaders to survive is to have people working with them who know more about what they do than do the leaders themselves. The people who run the machines, make the tests, sell the products, process the orders, deliver the services—the ones who actually do the work—know more about the technical requirements and other demands of their jobs than their supervisors know or can ever possibly know.

- The response time needed to ensure customer satisfaction (one major key to an organization's success) cannot be achieved unless the people who are in most direct contact with their customers make their own decisions without recourse to the directions of higher authority.

- People are ultimately their own bosses. It is when they view goals and standards as their own that they perform at their best.

Sustained superior performance is in the hands of the individual performers. All workers have control over how much energy they will put into a task. Most workers have *a lot* of control over which tasks they will do and how much time they will put into them. How this discretionary energy and time is used marks the difference between the committed and the uncommitted.

We know that people are more likely to use their discretionary energy and time to pursue organizational goals when (1) they have greater clarity about these goals and their importance, (2) they can exert influence over these goals, (3) they are more competent to achieve these goals, and (4) they receive more appreciation for working tirelessly to achieve these goals.

Coaching is an effective alternative to leading by control. In fact it is the antithesis of managing performance by trying to control people. Coaching helps create people who exercise their own self-control, and who are committed to excel in their own performance. Coaching, therefore, is your key to trusting and leading people—not controlling them. It is your key to involving people in both *what* needs to happen and *how* it will be accomplished. In Chapter 1, Coaching for Commitment, the many ways that coaching is a leadership function particularly suited to building commitment are described.

Overview of This Book

This book contains nine chapters.

Chapter 1: Coaching for Commitment. Chapter 1 explores the meaning and definition of coaching and commitment; discusses the visible evidence of such commitment; and shows how coaching occupies a central and dominant role for building commitment in others.

Chapter 2: The Coach Role. This chapter introduces *coach* as a distinct role from that of *manager, instructor, and mentor.* It also discusses the mental shift that must occur and the idea of being *egoless* in order to operate in the *coach role.*

Chapter 3: The Coaching Process. This chapter provides an overview of the four components that make up the coaching process and how they all work together. These elements are illustrated by the Coaching Prism.

Chapter 4: Trust. Establishing and building trust is the most important aspect of coaching. The focus here is on how to build and maintain trust by being honest, authentic, accountable, and respectful.

Chapter 5: The InDiCom Coaching Model. One key component of the coaching process is the InDiCom coaching model, with its corresponding stages and goals. The model is a recipe for having a coaching conversation and gaining commitment from the person being coached (PBC).

Chapter 6: CLEAR Coaching Skills. Another part of the coaching process are specific coaching skills, which can and should be used throughout all of the stages of the InDiCom coaching model. These coaching skills are represented by the acronym CLEAR: Challenge, Listen, Encourage, Ask, and Refine.

Chapter 7: Plan to Coach. This chapter focuses on performance coaching conversations, note-taking, channels of coaching, and tools for coaches. Worksheets are provided for planning your performance coaching conversations and for taking notes during your coaching conversations.

Chapter 8: The Complete Coaching Conversation. Coaching is a conversation that is logically and psychologically satisfying for the person being coached. This chapter ties everything together by providing multiple coaching conversation samples including two coaching moment conversations and one email conversation. These examples demonstrate the skills and techniques learned in the previous chapters.

Chapter 9: Creating a Coaching for Commitment Culture. Leaders now face the challenge of creating a Coaching for Commitment culture in which coaching becomes a welcomed and embraced role within teams. This chapter addresses what a Coaching for Commitment culture looks like, at the team or organizational level, how to create a value proposition for coaching, how to create a Coaching for Commitment culture—including a guide for creating an action plan—and how to gain commitment to creating a Coaching for Commitment culture.

CHAPTER 1

Coaching for Commitment

"Coaching is not just a function; it is a state of mind!"
—Amy Zehnder, Ph.D., PCC

GO AHEAD, We dare you! Find a good definition of coaching that you can easily remember. It's like trying to define leadership. There are hundreds of definitions out there, each one with a different mix of verbs and adjectives, each one trying to include statements about ownership, action items, and empowerment. You know the drill. Put some fancy definition together that nobody remembers or is capable of repeating without reading it, and you have a best seller! So, here it is. A definition of coaching in its most simplified, unglamorous form:

Coaching is all about the person being coached (PBC)!

Successful Coaching: A Working Definition

For those of you who would like a more comprehensive definition of coaching, one that you can sink your teeth into, here it is:

Successful coaching is a conversation of self-discovery that follows a logical process and leads to superior performance, commitment to sustained growth, and positive relationships.

All successful coaching conversations are pointed toward improving performance and ensuring a commitment to sustained superior performance and growth. These results can only be achieved through self-discovery on the part of the person being coached (PBC). Another outcome of successful coaching is the strengthening or improvement of positive relationships. One fundamental assumption of this book is that coaching can and should happen with top performers as often as under-performers.

You are coaching any time you help the PBC to close a gap in acuity, expertise, performance, or proficiency. Coaching is taking place whenever you assist another person in some sort of self-discovery. You are coaching when you help people find their own creative solutions. You are coaching when you help people discover new ways of thinking. You are coaching when you encourage people to find ways to maintain or improve their performance or to reach new stretch goals. You are coaching when you affirm others' commitment to personal development and acknowledge their successes.

Coaching occurs any time a personal and mutual interaction takes place by which the PBC experiences growth or ah-ha moments. Ah-ha moments happen when a light bulb comes on for someone you are coaching as a result of a personal revelation or discovery.

Coaching conversations can be both informal and formal. Informal coaching interactions are sometimes referred to as "coaching moments." Coaching moments typically last from two to ten minutes. They are quick coaching conversations that reaffirm the PBC is on the right track. They can occur after a formal coaching conversation has occurred. Most often, coaching moments are used to touch base, notice improvement, validate effort, or quickly redirect from a previous performance coaching conversation (based on the PBC's action plan). Formal coaching interactions typically last thirty to ninety minutes. In this book you will be introduced to the three-stage InDiCom coaching model, a set of five CLEAR coaching skills, and ways to plan for your coaching. These are applicable to both informal and formal coaching conversations. For a better understanding, Table 1.1 defines what coaching is and is not.

Table 1.1. Coaching Is/Is Not

COACHING IS	COACHING IS NOT
Accountability	A one-time event
Asking	Assuming
Caring	Avoidance
Clarifying	Blaming
Direct	Controlling
Discovering	Disciplinary Action
Egoless	Discouraging
Empowering	Leading
Encouraging	Limited
Listening	Prescriptive
Mutual	Reactive
Open-ended	Restrictive
Possibilities	Rigid
Positive	Sarcastic
Powerful	Solving
Proactive	Talking
Relevant	Telling
Supportive	Touchy-Feely
What *they* think!	What *you* think!

Coaching Works

The first reason for the ever-growing popularity of coaching, and possibly your interest in reading this book, is that coaching works! It is a proven strategy for creating sustained growth and achieving superior performance of individual, teams, and whole organizations. Testamonials to the value of coaching can be found in one or more business and training publications every month. Every performance function of every organization has benefited from coaching for as long as people have shared information about performance and how to improve it.

Not only does coaching work, but the reasons why it works are plentiful:

- Leaders need coaching skills to manage change.

- Executives need coaching skills to foster decision-making authority in others.

- Team leaders need coaching skills to support the development and performance of their teams.

- Sales managers need coaching skills because every sales person is successful in his or her own way.

- Customer service is improved by coaching people on how to respond to the expectations, jubilations, and irritations of their customers.

- Administrators need coaching skills to more effectively work with colleagues and co-workers.

- Teachers need coaching skills to work better with colleagues and students.

On-the-job training, mentoring, leading, managing, whatever the topic or role—in today's world—people need to have coaching skills.

Coaching is not dated; it is as current as you reading this book right now. Many organizations have found that coaching is the key to maintaining the competitive advantage in the marketplace. Coaching individuals who have made a psychological commitment to take actions that are in alignment with organizational objectives is a powerful way for organizations to achieve phenomenal results. Through coaching, individuals and organizations achieve maximum performance.

The Meaning of Commitment

A central theme of this book is that commitment is the key to superior performance and that coaching is the strategy for building that commitment. First, it is useful to clarify what commitment means.

One definition of Commitment found in the Merriam-Webster online dictionary is as follows:

> **Main Entry: com·mit·ment: Function: noun. 2 a: an agreement or pledge to do something in the future.. b: something pledged c: the state or an instance of being obligated or emotionally impelled <a commitment to a cause>**

This suggests that commitment is not just the physical act of follow-through, but also an emotional necessity or obligation.

An independent study conducted by Kinlaw (1991) determined the characteristics of superior teams. One dominant characteristic of superior teams was that team members felt "committed." People on superior teams described themselves as:

- Being focused.
- Looking forward to going to work.
- Caring about results and how well the team did.
- Taking it quite personally when the team did not meet its goals.
- Making personal sacrifices to make sure the team succeeded.
- Being determined to succeed.
- Never giving up.

Each of these things speaks to a level of commitment from the team's members.

The following is a typical example of what commitment looked like to a drafter in a design shop:

> "Coming to work in our shop means coming to work. We meet our schedules and we expect a completed design to be just that, complete. We take it very personally when our customer wants to make modifications when we submit our final. It means that we didn't do a good enough job staying in touch at every step from concept to finished product."

Commitment follows clarity and meaning. People need to connect what they do to some larger whole. They need to know how what they do contributes to their organization's success. They need to see the big picture.

Commitment, like motivation, is not something that you can observe directly. You infer that it exists because of what people do. You say that people are "committed" when they demonstrate over and over again their determination to do their best and their unwillingness to give up in the face of obstacles. Committed people in organizations are tied intellectually and emotionally to the values and goals of the organization. Committed people know what they are doing, and they believe that what they are doing is important. People cannot become committed to what is vague or trivial.

Some years ago, Dennis Kinlaw (1999) was consulting to a division of the old "Ma Bell" system and had an opportunity to observe firsthand the commitment of employees to perform consistently at their very best. It was obvious that one reason these employees demonstrated such commitment was that they had such a clear understanding of what was important and stayed focused on it. What was important became obvious whenever he asked any employee what his or her job was. Whether these employees were in purchasing or installation, or members of a line crew—their answers were the same: "My job is dial tone." These employees were committed to the one overarching goal (shared vision) of the company. They believed that giving the customer dial tone and restoring dial tone took precedence over everything else. Dial tone was the symbol for a working phone system. They understood the goal, and they had no question that it was of supreme importance.

Today, many companies may have a similar goal centered on connectivity: "Our goal is Internet connectivity." This is especially true for online companies and companies that rely heavily on online services.

A common complaint among leaders about the service and administrative functions in their organizations is that the people in these functions are "not committed to the bottom line" or they "don't have the big picture." These leaders are often right, but continually do not see their own part in the problem.

"Pushing paper," as a job duty, can range anywhere from filing, to keeping funding requests flowing smoothly, to ensuring every employee is paid on time. These are big jobs! And they are more likely to be done well if the people doing them see it clearly as a step in fulfilling the company's mission. If you want "support" staff to share the same commitment to the company's bottom line, then you must show them how their services and products contribute to that bottom line. A job is only a job until it becomes a commitment, and commitment is only possible when people see the *meaning* in what they do.

Building Commitment Through Coaching

Figure 1.1 displays four critical conditions that contribute to the development of commitment. People tend to become fully committed to do their best all of the time to the degree that they:

- Are clear about core values and performance goals.
- Have influence over what they do.
- Have the competence to perform the jobs that are expected of them.
- Are appreciated for their performance.

Coaching is a particularly powerful way to develop these conditions for individuals and teams. Each of these conditions is explained, including the special contribution that successful coaching makes in creating each.

Being Clear

An accepted fundamental condition for building the commitment of people in organizations is that they are clear about the organization's foundation or core values and its primary goals. When people are clear about the organization's values and goals, they can align their

Figure 1.1. Four Critical Conditions for Building Commitment

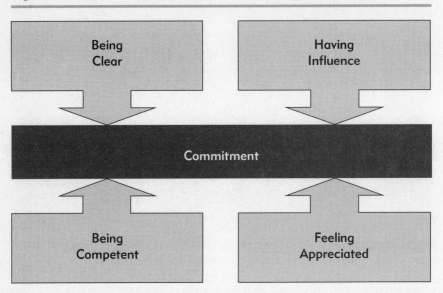

work to these goals, which in turn provides role clarity and a sense of belonging.

Ambivalence and confusion are the enemies of commitment. Values that are clearly communicated, adhered to, and reinforced by the behaviors of leaders give people the basis for making decisions when there are no specific rules for making such decisions. Knowing what the real values, goals, and vision of an organization are provides members a framework within which a vast variety of behaviors are possible, and it helps people resolve conflicts over priorities. When values and goals are not clear, commitment cannot be built, and performance suffers.

Coaching resolves questions about values and goals through a process of collaboration and consensus. It is easy to see the importance of clarifying goals when looking at teams. Team members often begin their tasks with high energy and determination, but problems can undermine progress and commitment. One of the most common problems a team can experience is changing priorities. When teams change priorities, they must resolve new problems, make decisions, analyze data, reprioritize, and strategize how to move forward. If during this process they continually have to change directions or digress from the goal, the energy level drops, discouragement sets in, and members begin to feel that they are wasting time and become frustrated. At this point, the team needs someone to address resistance, encourage forward movement, and ultimately facilitate the team's ability to reconnect the new priorities with core values, overall team goals, and individual roles. The team needs someone to help them recommit—that is, they need a coach. The best coach in these cases is often a team member.

Issuing goals and publishing values in a work group or organization does not automatically result in exerting practical influence over what people do. Some of the more frequent kinds of conversation that take place among peers and between workers and their appointed leaders are those in which people raise questions about what is important, what should be done first, when a job is considered complete, and how to fulfill expectations. All such questions present opportunities for coaching interactions.

Having Influence

Many of you have seen how people perform when they are consistently denied any say-so in their jobs and are expected to follow unquestionably the decisions of their leaders.

Leaders who deny people influence receive what they deserve. People who do *exactly* what they are told to do—nothing more, nothing less.

Every person in any organization is presented countless opportunities to encourage others to explore and analyze the various problems they must solve about their work and about their relationships with others. The power of self-managed teams comes from the opportunity that members have to influence the performance of teammates (and their managers) by the free use of their own knowledge and skills.

It takes discipline to encourage people to exert influence. Think of the many ways that people routinely inhibit others from fully expressing an idea or thinking independently. An example of this is demonstrated in the following story:

> Gary was at his mother-in-law's house and she asked him to check the oil in her car. Like all good sons-in-law, he didn't hesitate. He immediately went into the garage to check the oil in Shelly's car (something that he'd done in his own car many times). A few minutes later, Shelly went into the garage and noticed that Gary was looking very closely at the end of the dip stick. She quickly informed Gary that he wasn't doing it "right" by saying, "No Gary, you have to wipe it off first and put it back in to get a good reading." He bristled with resistance and replied, "You can tell me what to do [check the oil], or how to do it [wipe it off first and put it back in], but not both!"

All too often, managers do the same thing to their employees. They tell them both *what to do* and *how to do it* leaving no room for independent thought or application of knowledge and skill, or they come into a situation midstream, make assumptions, and act without having all the information. In the previous example, how did Shelly know that Gary hadn't already wiped the dipstick? He may have been checking the level accurately, but she didn't take the time to find out.

The words, "You can tell me what to do, or how to do it, but not both," make a compelling point. By telling people both *what* and *how* to do something, you stifle creativity and diminish their ability to influence. If you only tell people *what* to do, they will have input and creativity in figuring out *how* it should get done. If you only tell people *how* something should be completed, are you willing to live with *what* they come up with?

Every successful coaching conversation is about how the PBC can influence the *what* and the *how*. As a coach, you will want to make full use of what the PBC knows, thinks, and discovers. Coaching helps people gain new insight, which in turn helps them to discover new opportunities to exert influence over their jobs and their lives. It gives

them choices, reinforces self-esteem, encourages innovation
for a feeling of self-sufficiency, pride, and the ability to hav
over their own outcomes. Disciplined coaches help others identify their
own needs and help them shape the way those needs are met. Coaching often helps others set their own performance expectations and
career goals.

When you observe successful coaches in action, you will hear them
using the following kinds of phrases, calculated to help others influence their own outcomes:

- "How do you think you should go about resolving this issue?"
- "What sorts of things have you tried so far?"
- "How can you influence this?"
- "What is within your control?"
- "What resources can you identify that can help?"

Being Competent

Another condition that produces commitment in people to do their
best all of the time is that they feel competent. People do not naturally
want to fail, but they will often try to avoid the tasks that they think
they cannot do. If you want commitment from people, you must
ensure they have the tools, resources, ability, and willingness to succeed in their jobs. Ensuring that people have the knowledge, skill,
experience, tools, and resources to perform and confidence to perform
are critical elements to building competency in others. Coaching
accomplishes both of these.

Coaching is the means by which people feel supported in learning the
new knowledge and skills they need to do their best. Although
the knowledge and skill is mostly obtained through training, on-the-
job experience, and by working with subject-matter experts, coaching supports the individualized learning curve and helps people
find the confidence to test their new skills and take the initiative to
learn more.

Here are a few of the reasons that successful coaching is such a powerful strategy for building competence. The personal, interactive nature of coaching:

- Makes it easy for people to succeed by helping them break their learning into small increments.

- Provides the PBC with the opportunity to demonstrate and verify new learning during the process of being coached.

- Gives people personal encouragement and support, which increases the probability of success.

- Makes it possible for people to fail safely and to learn from mistakes.

- Challenges people to attempt more and more difficult tasks.

Coaching is the one sure way that you can find out exactly what others do not know and what they need to know—simply by asking the right questions. Coaching is also a way to give support and to reassure people who are taking on new tasks. Coaching facilitates the process of learning, because it is timely and focuses exactly on what each individual or team needs. Successful learning, in turn, builds confidence.

Feeling Appreciated

Finally, to achieve commitment one must feel appreciated. One of Kinlaw's theories was that if you want to know how people feel about their organization and their work, check the bathrooms. In one company the bathrooms were always immaculate. The whole place looked as though it had been scrubbed with a toothbrush. One time the "being cleaned" sign was out and the janitor was cleaning, so Dr. Kinlaw took the chance to thank him and to tell him what a great job he was doing. Then he asked him, "What makes you do it? Why do you do such a great job?" The janitor answered, "Because I know everyone appreciates it being nice."

Kinlaw later found out that a senior leader in the building set the example of making people feel appreciated; he routinely took special care to thank the janitor for his work. Once, the senior leader, after preparing a letter of appreciation, summoned the janitor to the fourth floor. Because the janitor didn't know why he had been called to the executive floor, he was pleasantly surprised when the vice president of the company presented him with the letter.

So how can you predict an organization's performance? The most reliable variables are employees' perceptions of clarity, fairness, responsiveness, involvement, and appreciation. Even an employee's workspace can tell you something about the environment. The variable that employees are often least positive about is appreciation.

Everyone can learn something about appreciation. Sometimes what people do not know about appreciation is mind-boggling. During a seminar one participant said to another participant, "Say, Kevin, you mentioned during our last discussion that you make it a point to write people thank-you notes when they go out of their way or do something special. Just what sort of things do you say in those notes?" Kevin replied, "I always try to acknowledge the specific behavior or the action, along with the positive impact it had on others. For example, "Alison, the feedback you provided on my last report was extremely helpful because I knew exactly what I needed to change. Thank you for being so clear." In response to this, one tough-minded leader in the class said, "Well, where I come from, the appreciation that you get for doing a good job is that you get to keep your job." Surprisingly, this mindset is still common; many managers believe that they do not need to continually thank people because what they are doing is part of their job description. Being "too busy" is another common excuse for not thanking employees for a job well done. This bull-headedness may sound good to some, but it doesn't work! Not if you are looking for commitment. Commitment to superior performance is a function of clarity, competence, influence, and appreciation. People work the best when they believe that what they do counts for something to someone else—especially the people with whom they work.

Among the many things that successful coaching accomplishes is that it communicates personal appreciation. During your coaching conversations, you will encourage the PBC and show appreciation for his or her ideas. You will acknowledge and celebrate the PBC's successes and make him or her feel that you are supportive and care about the success, and that you do so from a perspective larger than just "bottom line" thinking. You will make people feel appreciated by valuing their ideas, their self-discoveries, their growth, their action plans, and their commitment to action. Successful coaches use every opportunity to emphasize the strengths and accomplishments of the PBC. Appreciation is often shown by the words you use during your coaching conversations. Common expressions found in extended coaching interactions include the following:

- "Thanks for putting such effort in to working through this problem. It will save the team a lot of time."

- "Your ideas were fabulous and should get you to where you want to go."

- "I know it wasn't easy to look at the problems you are having on your team, and I do appreciate your being so candid in talking about it."

- "I like how you are not letting this small setback cast a shadow over all of the good work you've done."

Commitment, in summary, is the dominating key to superior performance. There are four critical conditions that determine whether the PBC becomes fully committed to continually do his or her best:

1. Being Clear: The PBC is clear about core values and performance goals.

2. Having Influence: The PBC has influence over *what* he or she does and *how* he or she does it.

3. Being Competent: The PBC has the competencies to perform the job that is expected of him or her.

4. Feeling Appreciated: The PBC is appreciated for his or her performance.

Every conversation is potentially a coaching conversation. It is a chance to discover new ways to look at things, new ways to accomplish goals, and opportunities to create ah-ha moments that help people see things from a different perspective. It is a chance to reaffirm and reinforce the PBC's alignment to the organization's core values. It is a chance to hear ideas and involve others in the processes of planning and problem solving. And more importantly, it is a chance to say "thank you for a job well done."

Coaching for Commitment

Coaching is something you do *with* people, not *to* them. Coaching is considered successful when people commit to their ideas and put their words into action. More than that, your goal as a coach should be to commit to modeling the coaching behaviors and skills presented in this book. Imagine the power of many coaches working together to build commitment to sustained growth and superior performance— through people.

Coaching Moment

Current Reality: Use a 1 to 3 scale to answer the following questions:

1 = not committed at all   2 = somewhat committed   3 = totally committed

1. What is your personal level of commitment to coaching?
2. What is your personal level of commitment to creating a coaching culture?
3. (if applicable) What is your manager's level of commitment to coaching?
4. (if applicable) What is your manager's level of commitment to creating a coaching culture?
5. (if applicable) What is your organization's level of commitment to coaching?

6. (if applicable) What is your organization's level of commitment to creating a coaching culture?

Ideal State: Where do you think the level of commitment should be for each?

Action Plan: What is your part in maintaining the current level (if above 1) or achieving a higher level? How can you influence others?

Chapter Summary

Simple Coaching Definition:

Coaching is all about the person being coached (PBC)!

Comprehensive Coaching Definition:

Successful coaching is a conversation of self-discovery that follows a logical process and leads to superior performance, commitment to sustained growth, and positive relationships.

Commitment is a key strategy for obtaining phenomenal organizational results. Commitment is created when the people being coached:

- Are clear about core values and performance goals.

- Have influence over *what* they do and *how* they do it.

- Have the competencies to perform the jobs that are expected of them.

- Are appreciated for their performance.

Coaching is considered successful when the coach:

- Helps the PBC to commit to his or her ideas and put them into action.

- Effectively models coaching for commitment skills and behaviors.

CHAPTER 2

The Coach Role

"Coaching takes a great deal of time, professionalism, and commitment. It also takes just the right personality and inner strength to be a great coach."

—Alison House, O.D.

JUST AS COACHES who live and breathe coaching must sometimes make a conscious shift to a non-coaching role when dealing with others; non-coaches and new coaches alike must make a similar shift in thinking before approaching a "coaching conversation." This book may change the way you have always thought about coaching!

The most recent controversy around coaching is what actually constitutes coaching. Is every interaction you have with another person considered coaching? The simple answer is, no.

Coaching is distinct in nature and is set apart from other interactions because it is based solely on the *needs* of the person being coached (PBC) and uses a clearly defined process throughout the interaction. Not every interaction is coaching, and yet over time people have applied the coaching label to everything from leadership to consulting and from medicine to management. It seems that everything is being labeled as coaching these days, which is why a definition of

Coaching for Commitment is so hard to discern. To further complicate matters, most people associate coaching with sports. This book is *not* about sports coaching. The Coaching for Commitment kind of coaching—the kind that is *all about the person being coached*—is not just a function or position title; it is a state of mind.

Does this mean then that leaders, managers, business owners, and consultants don't make good coaches? Absolutely not! What it does mean is that in order to shift to the *coach role* it is fundamental for them to:

- Be willing to adopt the philosophy of coaching when they are in the *coach role*.
- Make a distinction between when they are coaching and when they are using another role (*manage*, *mentor*, or *instructor*).
- Make a clear shift to a coaching state of mind.

Coaching for Commitment has a companion assessment—Coaching Skills Inventory (CSI). The CSI: Self identifies the role you gravitate toward most often, your coaching gap, and what skills could be improved to increase your coaching effectiveness. It is recommended that you take the CSI before reading this chapter so that you have a starting point for understanding the four roles presented here and a basis for understanding the ideas and concepts used throughout this book. For those who want to explore how others perceive them, a CSI: Observer tool is also available. Copies of the CSI: Self and CSI: Observer can be obtained through Pfeiffer (www.pfeiffer.com).

Role Distinctions—What and How

Conversations occur for any variety of reasons. Most conversations include *what* and *how*. One person communicates to the other person the *what*.

What is defined as the results, outcomes, goals, or objectives expected of the other person. For example, a customer service group may have a target of returning 98 percent of customer voicemails within twenty-four hours.

How is defined as the behaviors and actions (actionable items) that a person takes to achieve the *what*. For example, using the same customer service group, the *how* for one person may be checking his voicemail between calls, making notes, and then returning all calls at the end of the day. Another customer service representative may use a different approach.

In this section, we will review how the *what* and *how* are handled in each role: *manager*, *mentor*, and *instructor*. Each role has its place and provides value based on the type of interaction and needs of the conversation at hand. The goal is not to eliminate any role, but rather to increase your awareness of the shift that needs to occur as you transition from *manager*, *instructor*, or *mentor* into the *coach role*.

Manager Role

The *manager role* is more than a job title or position; anyone can play the *manager role*. The *manager role* is executed when only the *what* of the task, project, or event is communicated to others. An example of a non-manager playing the *manager role* is when an employee takes responsibility for organizing a company picnic; he or she will manage *what* needs to be accomplished and rely on others to help carry out the *how*.

Great managers provide the *what* to employees and allow them autonomy to figure out *how* to get it done. For example, a sales manager may provide *what* needs to happen by stating a target: "We need to hit 90 percent of our sales goals by September." Then, the manager encourages employees, trusts their expertise, and lets them figure out *how* to make the 90 percent happen.

A manager . . .

- Identifies expectations, standards, processes, and results and holds employees accountable to them.
- Allows autonomy in achieving results.
- Creates an environment in which employees are allowed to make mistakes and learn from them.

- Encourages innovation.
- Is flexible and open to new ideas.
- Encourages employees to expand on existing skills and build upon strengths.
- Allows employees to figure out how to be successful and supports their efforts.
- Helps employees figure out how to resolve performance deficits.
- Supports behaviors or actions that lead to improved interactions with team members and greater productivity.

Mentor Role

Mentors provide the *how*, not the *what*. The *what* is provided by the person seeking the mentor's expertise. For example, if the person being mentored wants to know *what* he or she needs to do to get noticed within the company, he or she would approach the mentor seeking information on *how* to make it happen. In this situation, the mentor might say something like the following, "If you really want the senior staff to notice you, get in front of them more often by volunteering to do the monthly budget presentation."

A mentor . . .

- Provides advice and support to a person who is interested in career planning or advancement.
- Helps develop a person's political savvy and sensitivity to organizational culture and environment.
- Provides persons with proactive approaches for managing their own careers.
- Suggests an educational course of action or provides information and resources for professional development.
- Tells a person how to prepare so that one day he or she can move into the mentor's job.

Instructor Role

Instructors provide people with both the *what* and the *how*. Providing both the *what and* the *how* is often used by instructors to teach people new skills, and by consultants who are hired to provide both the *what* and the *how* from an expert perspective. Instructors provide both *what* and *how* by way of teaching, training, tutoring, consulting, and presenting.

An instructor . . .

- Provides knowledge to help someone become proficient.

- Teaches skills that make others successful.

- Provides instruction to new or less experienced persons.

- Presents information, processes, or steps to perform a task.

- Provides "expert" advice on what to do and how to do it.

Shift Happens!

Before looking at the *coach role*, it is important to first look at a shift that will occur in accordance with Figure 2.1.

Let Go of What and How

To help you succeed in the *coach role*, enter a coach state of mind by making a mental *shift* to coach. When you let go of **both** the *what* and the *how*, you enter the world of coaching. It is at this precise point where you change your thinking from being the one to provide answers and solutions to being the one who draws *all* of the answers and solutions from the PBC. In essence, you become *egoless* (without ego or bias), deriving your satisfaction from making others the experts and helping them achieve success through coaching, rather than being successful by fixing, doing, or being the expert yourself.

What happens once you truly make the shift to coach will be amazing!

Figure 2.1. Role Model

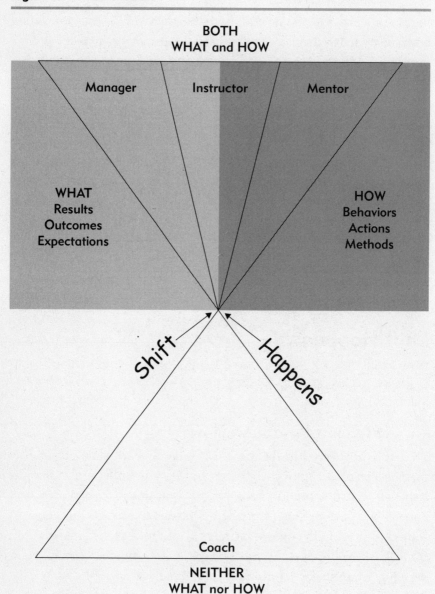

BOTH
WHAT and HOW

Manager   Instructor   Mentor

WHAT
Results
Outcomes
Expectations

HOW
Behaviors
Actions
Methods

Shift   Happens

Coach

NEITHER
WHAT nor HOW

Coach Biases

Making the shift to the *coach* role requires that you eliminate biases and become *egoless*. Simple in concept, difficult in application.

The need to be *egoless* in a coaching conversation stems in part from the fact that people have so many biases. People will not feel satisfied in a coaching conversation or relationship with you if they sense that they are being subjected to your opinions and biases. Coaching conversations will not be a positive experience for people if they are based largely on your subjective perceptions, opinions, inferences, or assumptions about the other person's attitudes or motives.

Biases stem from your personal values, prejudices, judgments, and the filters you use to view the world. You bring to the table a set of core values, ethics, and rules for living your life and working. Your values are one of the many things that make you unique. You living by your values is easy. Expecting others to live by your values has about as much chance of success as winning the big lottery jackpot. In coaching, your challenge will be to allow the PBC to honor, live by, and seek solutions in accordance with his or her values, not yours.

If one of the outcomes of coaching is the ability for the PBC to solve his or her own issues or figure out his or her own path, then doesn't it stand to reason that keeping your values out of the mix is the prudent approach? One would think so, yet time and time again, we hear different versions of the same conversation in working with new coaches. The following is one example that can occur when looking at career development opportunities with the PBC. This one is about a manager, Kao, who was new to the department, and who came in just before the year-end review process with her new team. Elwin is one of her new direct reports and she has decided to have a one-on-one "coaching" conversation with him.

COACH/KAO: "Hello, Elwin! Good to see you! I'd like to follow up from our year-end review conversation and explore developmental opportunities with you for the upcoming year."

PBC/ELWIN: "Thanks, Kao, I appreciate that, but I don't know what you mean. I am already performing well above my peers. Isn't that good enough?"

COACH/KAO: "Of course it is! In fact, it is so good, that I want to see you move up in the organization."

PBC/ELWIN: "I am pretty happy where I am, Kao. I like my job, you, and the people I work with. I don't have any interest in leaving the department or moving up any time soon."

COACH/KAO: "Elwin, I'm not sure I understand. You are one of my best employees and you don't want to move up in the company? Don't you want to make more money?"

PBC/ELWIN: "Money isn't everything."

COACH/KAO (getting frustrated): "Do you mean to tell me that you are not interested in leaving this role or getting promoted?"

What is going on here? What values does Kao have that Elwin does not share with her? What might Elwin's values be? The fact that Elwin doesn't have an interest in moving up in the company really bothers Kao. Why? Because of her biases.

In debriefing Kao it turns out that money is very important to her. She is on the corporate fast track and is highly motivated to move up as fast as she can. She cannot understand why such a good employee (like Elwin) doesn't want to be on the same track with her. She also admits that she is a bit jealous of Elwin's life-balance and his ability to set boundaries. Elwin goes home almost every day at 5 P.M. on the dot and rarely works overtime. She does plenty of overtime. Kao shared that she is thirty-ish, single, and without a family, while Elwin is over fifty with a wife and two college-aged kids. Kao freely admits that her life is her job, thus it is only natural for her to assume that it should be that way for others.

If given the opportunity, Elwin might have shared that his family is his first priority. He was on the corporate fast track in his past, working long hours, eating on the run, never home, and under a great deal of stress. Elwin had a personal wake-up call that caused him to rethink his priorities. When it comes to work, he now chooses the path of least resistance so that he will be there to see his daughters graduate from high school. He now prides himself on making it to every one of his daughters' softball games and swim meets instead of being promoted at work. Elwin's wife works part-time, which means there is a reasonable amount of financial security—thus his comment, "Money isn't everything." He doesn't know Kao well enough yet to have shared all of this information with her. Besides, she didn't give him a chance! From this example, you can see how powerful biases are. When you superimpose your biases onto a PBC during a coaching conversation, it's not really coaching.

Because the people you coach do not see the world through your eyes, with your values and biases, you will need to learn to step outside of your own viewpoint to embrace, encourage, and accept the views, needs, and solutions of the people you coach.

Biased or prejudiced comments coming from the coach will typically yield a defensive reaction by the PBC, often resulting in the PBC shutting down, becoming disengaged, mentally distracted, and communicating less. Unfortunately, you may never know you said anything wrong because the PBC likely will not tell you. He or she will just stop communicating openly. Keep in mind, any biased, prejudiced, or narrow-minded comments made by you will destroy the effectiveness of your coaching.

Trust, the core of all coaching relationships, is destroyed whenever the PBC feels that he or she is being treated in an arbitrary or high-handed manner. As soon as the PBC feels your biases or prejudices have entered the conversation, you have lost your credibility as a coach and the fundamental factor for a successful coaching relationship, trust.

The following are examples (from our archives) of undesirable biased or prejudiced comments that should not be used in a coaching conversation:

- "It must be a cultural thing."
- "You're too young. . . ."

- "I dislike people who are late all of the time." (To someone who is late.)

- "Have you thought about changing your hairstyle or dress in order to fit in better?"

- "The key to getting ahead is to work long hours and weekends. You have to give the company your heart and soul to have any chance of being successful."

- "The rest of us are pitching in and staying late; what's your problem?"

- "I'll do it myself. You're obviously already on vacation."

To remain unbiased and open-minded, you must first be self-aware. When you have strong opinions about something, or beliefs that differ from others' beliefs, it is even more important that you put the effort in to remain unbiased, be non-judgmental, and seek first to understand and accept people for who they are. Using comments like the following can help:

- "Help me to understand your perspective on this."

- "My opinion doesn't matter here; what matters is yours. How do you feel about your decision?"

- "Please tell me what you are thinking."

- "I have ideas, but I'd like to hear yours."

Egoless

How can you eliminate biases? The best strategy for eliminating or preventing coaching biases is to focus on being *egoless*.

Being *egoless* means that you coach based on the needs of the PBC. You don't take things personally, you don't blame, and you don't make assumptions; you take your own goals, drive, aspirations, and emotions out of the mix. It means that, rather than being the rewarded problem solver or winner, you feed your ego by finding ways to help elevate the PBC to that status.

Being *egoless* also means you check your ego at the door, and that you are aware of your biases, your agenda, or any hidden agendas that you may have when in the *coach role*. As the coach, you do not lead discussions based on your pre-set solutions and do not ask questions that direct the PBC toward one set of answers (which are likely to be yours). Solutions and answers are for the PBC to discover for him- or herself.

Being *egoless* is the most unselfish, unbiased self you can bring to the table. Once you make the conversation about the PBC and not about you, the outcome will be more productive.

Think of an *egoless* coach as one who keeps his or her own filters, prejudices, and values out of the situation. One who does not force the problem/issue into one mindset or frame of reference. Even if you need to conduct a coaching conversation that is based on poor performance, your role is to present the performance issue or deficiency area from a neutral, unbiased, non-prejudiced, *egoless* viewpoint. In these cases, always be aware of your tone and/or body language.

Coaches are self-aware to the point that they are able to remain completely objective and do not make judgments (right/wrong/indifferent) about the PBC, their suggestions, feelings, emotions, ideas, or solutions.

Being *egoless* means that you don't take any part of the coaching conversation personally. In other words, if you remove your ego from the interaction, you cannot be harmed by words or attitude. In addition, you, as the coach, must be willing to be wrong, accept that fact gracefully, and move on.

You will discover that remaining *egoless* becomes much more difficult when the coaching conversation elicits strong emotional responses or reactions. While most coaching conversations are viewed as positive, telling someone that he or she is not performing a task at a satisfactory level will rarely be received without some degree of apprehension, defensiveness, and/or anger. In cases where a coach needs to address a performance issue, the PBC will often perceive the conversation (at least initially) as a reprimand.

During all coaching conversations, maintaining trust between you and the PBC is essential. This can be accomplished, in part, by remaining *egoless*.

Being *egoless* gets easier if you can keep one thing in mind, "It's all about the person being coached (PBC)!" If at first being *egoless* is hard for you, allow yourself the ability to rewind or take a do-over. You can do so verbally, "I would like to take back what I just said and rephrase it as . . ." or "Let me try that again." Above all, be honest with yourself and the PBC. Sometimes admission of imperfection on the part of the coach can do wonders to stimulate the trust environment. It means you are human. It also means that you model the way in allowing and admitting to mistakes. If at any point during your coaching conversations you find yourself not being *egoless*, mentally stop yourself and recommit to the PBC.

Clear the Clutter

Part of getting into the coach mindset includes clearing mental and physical clutter. Be very clear in your mind that you are about to conduct a coaching conversation. Coaching is not a casual conversation. It takes concentrated mental energy and effort that is draining yet revitalizing at the same time. Coaching is work.

Here are some suggestions for mentally getting ready to coach:

- Figure out a trick or technique for yourself that distinguishes when you are actually coaching. For example, one coach visualizes that she is in the audience and the person being coached (PBC) is on the stage under a spotlight; another mentally goes through the process of putting a coach baseball cap on.

- Use a physical/tangible item to remind you that you are coaching. Any time you are about to begin coaching, place this physical object near you to remind you that you are in coach-mode. For instance, a lamp turned on can serve the same purpose as the mental spotlight mentioned previously.

- A clock is not recommended, as you will be tempted to look
  at it and it may appear as though you are in a hurry to get
  through the session. Similarly, anything that you hold in
  your hand can be distracting if you choose to fidget with
  the item while you are trying to be attentive.

Mental and physical distractions can be huge detractors during a
coaching conversation. Be prepared to put aside your "stuff," all of it,
up to and including your piled-high desk, bad day, or your personal
challenges at the moment. Free your mind and clear the clutter.

Forget about multitasking, including answering or even looking at
your phone or email during your coaching conversations. Your job is
to convey to the PBC that he or she is the most important person in
your world for that moment in time. If you are in the habit of multitasking or doing several things at once, especially on conference calls
or when coaching by phone/virtually, make a commitment to stop
those activities while coaching.

Freeing your mind is mostly mental, but sometimes doing something physical can help. Here are some suggestions to help free your
mind before the coaching conversation:

- Close your eyes and count backwards slowly from twenty.

- Break yourself away from your work station. Go get a glass of
  water or coffee or do something to change your physical
  environment for a moment or two.

- If you've ever taken a yoga class, you understand the principles
  and benefits of deep breathing exercises that relax you and bring
  oxygen to the muscles and brain. Breathing in slowly and
  exhaling in a controlled manner for several breaths can relax
  you and clear your mind. Listen to the sound of your breath,
  trying to achieve a long inhale of at least eight to ten seconds
  and a controlled exhale of ten seconds or longer. About five or
  six full breaths should help you to feel more relaxed and in tune.
  (If you have breathing problems, check with your doctor first!)

If you're in the midst of your coaching conversation and your mind starts to drift, do your best to refocus the attention back on the PBC each time it occurs.

Clearing the clutter also means reducing the physical distractions that plague you at work and in your workspace. These are the things that cause you to turn your head and look away from the PBC momentarily or that make your ears perk up so that you miss that last sentence, critical link, or key element. The heaped-on desk, the cubicle environment, the radio down the way, your calendar glaring at you to remind you of a very important meeting in just one hour, the clamor of ticking clocks, pumped in white noise, you name it, the distractions are there!

Here are some suggestions to help you clear the clutter in your physical environment (consider these ideas when coaching in person or by phone):

- Close your appointment book or your calendar software.

- Forward your phone or set it to a one ring feature (and don't look at it if it rings.)

- Turn the sound off on your computer monitor so you don't hear those emails sneaking in or the next appointment reminder.

- Turn off your monitor, your cell phone, and any other gadgetry that may be tempting you to look at it, touch it, or use it.

- If your office is too cluttered, find a room with little visual distraction.

- If the office is too cluttered, go to the coffee shop, out for lunch, or for a walk.

- Clear off your desk or the table where you will be meeting in order to limit distraction and make the space clear and inviting.

- While coaching on the phone, try using a headset so that you can hear clearly. This also helps to block out at least one ear's worth of background noise. You can also use an earplug in the other ear.

- Do not check, send, or even think about looking at your email while coaching. You will be distracted.

- Find the things that distract you the most and either get rid of them or set them aside during your coaching conversation.

- Schedule coaching appointments on your calendar so your time is free and clear from interruptions.

Now that you know how to make the shift to coach—by letting go of the *what* and the *how*, eliminating biases, becoming *egoless*, and clearing away mental and physical distractions—let's explore who should coach, the value proposition for coaching, and the perspectives of a coach.

Coach Role

Coaching can be a mental challenge as you learn that you are no longer in control of, or providing, the *what* or the *how*. This concept is difficult to grasp for most people because they have been known, rewarded, promoted, and encouraged for being the one with all the answers (the expert). Most of us take pride in providing direction, guidance, solutions, explanations, and ideas. Put plain and simply, many of us just can't help ourselves from wanting to fill in all the blanks. In fact, we usually see this behavior as "helpful."

As you transition to the *coach role*, you will learn that the coach provides neither the *what* nor the *how* to the PBC. You may ask, "How is this possible?" Think of this in terms of what role each person plays in a coaching conversation. It's not that the *what* and *how* are completely absent from the coaching conversation, it's just that the PBC *owns* both of them, not you.

Although either person (coach or PBC) can begin any coaching conversation, the concept of the coach releasing control of the *what* and *how* is certainly *more* obvious when the PBC communicates the *why* of the conversation (*Why* are we having this coaching conversation?) to the coach. This typically occurs at the very beginning of the conversation. The PBC then communicates *what* he or she wants to have happen. It is then the coach's job to skillfully draw out of the PBC *how* to make it happen.

There are times when the coach will be the one communicating the *why* (*Why* are we having this coaching conversation?) to the PBC. This situation most often occurs with performance coaching conversations (see Chapter 7). During performance coaching, the coach gives the *why* and then works to get the PBC to take ownership so that the PBC can own the *what* and the *how*.

Examples:

PBC communicates WHY: "I've been meaning to talk with you. I'm working on improving my partnering ability and ran into something that I need help with."
In this example, you should help the PBC clearly define the goal (*what*) and determine *how* he or she will achieve it. If you launch into telling this person *how* to fix the problem, you have taken on the *mentor role*, not the *coach role*.

Coach communicates WHY: "I've noticed that you're not that comfortable in front of an audience, yet your role requires that you present information frequently. I know that you want to be successful in this area. How do you think you can become more comfortable presenting?"

A coach:

- Uses a coaching process to help the PBC identify *what* he or she needs to do and *how* to do it, then gain insight and move forward.

- Challenges the PBC's status quo.

- Listens more than talks.

- Encourages the PBC to take risks.

- Encourages the PBC to find his or her own solutions.

- Asks more than tells.

- Remains *egoless* and sets bias aside.

- Provides opportunity for exploration of new ideas.
- Provides clarity to the coaching conversation.

When to Coach

The *coach role* is best used for interactions that move the PBC forward, specifically when the PBC:

- Needs insight about his or her behavior and actions. (Sometimes gained through the use of 360-degree feedback assessments, discussed in greater detail in Chapter 7.)
- Is feeling stagnant, stuck, or has outgrown a role.
- Has a drive for greatness.
- Is not sure what is interfering with the ability to achieve some personal or professional goal.
- Needs to find a way to move forward or make progress.
- Is trying to move from average or good to better and best.
- Realizes that some technical, organizational, or other problem is blocking his or her performance or potential.
- Has a very difficult choice to make, such as the decision to take on a new role or new challenge.
- Needs help preparing for an upcoming difficult task, conversation, or presentation.

The coach's role is to help the PBC gain insight and understanding regarding the topic of conversation, not to solve the problem for him or her. In coaching conversations, the coach spends the majority of time (about 80 percent) listening and the remaining time (about 20 percent) asking mostly open-ended *coaching questions.* Many coaches struggle with not solving, or wanting to direct the conversation to their end. Coaching is often the role that people think they are in, when in reality they are more likely in one of the other roles (*manager, mentor,* or *instructor*). This is a common ah-ha that people have when taking the CSI and during coaching workshops.

Who Should Coach?

Coaching is not *just* a stand-alone profession. It can and should be used by anyone who interacts with people. Coaching can and should be a part of everybody's job! People who have assigned leadership roles should strive to become proficient in the *coach role*. Managers, when not playing the *manager* role, should know how to coach. People in every organization and in every position should have the opportunity to learn how to be a coach. Coaching does not depend on one's having a certain organizational position or title. It depends on having the desire to help others succeed and possessing the knowledge and skills that it takes to work through the process of a coaching conversation.

Benefits of Coaching—Value Proposition

Why coach? Coaching's value proposition is impressive. The return on investment (ROI) for coaching can be multiple times the initial investment, one study suggests up to 529 percent (Anderson, 2001) and another puts the figure at nearly six times the initial cost (Right Management Consultants, 2004a). If that isn't enough, coaching is set apart from all other roles because it targets the difference between what is and what is desired to be. Coaching uses the expertise, knowledge, skill, action, and commitment of the PBC to close the gap and reach success in accomplishing goals. But coaching does more than produce just an immediate result. Successful coaching achieves the long-term result of new and renewed commitment to superior performance, sustained growth, and continuous improvement while maintaining positive relationships, which ultimately creates high-performing individuals and teams and an increase in your bottom line.

Think of coaching as you would the "teach a man to fish" philosophy. At first, it may appear that the coaching process would take longer using this approach, but you will realize the opposite to be true. The end result will be less of your time spent answering questions and a PBC who is empowered, less dependent, and ultimately more productive.

In the end, a PBC who feels empowered and motivated to take action in a productive and targeted manner takes accountability by owning the situation, his or her behavior, and the outcomes. The PBC is responsible and accountable for both *what* needs to happen and *how* to make it happen. All of this because you, as the coach, expanded on the person's existing skills and built on his or her strengths.

Perspectives of a Coach

Coaches focus on:

- The PBC.
- The Process.
- The Gap.
- The Future.

Focus Is on the PBC

Coaching consists of conversations that are specific to the needs and interests of the PBC. Coaching is shaped by discovering what PBCs know, even if they do not yet realize that they know it. It is shaped by the coach who responds to the conversation that is immediately at hand, with no ulterior motives. Coaching is very individualized. Coaching people to discover new ways of seeing things is a highly interactive process of give-and-take in which the PBC defines *what* needs to happen and *how* to make it happen.

Focus on the needs of the PBC, not on yours. If you are driven by *your* needs, you can be overly critical and have a strong need to speak your mind or even tell someone off (especially during a performance coaching conversation). Any time you are emotionally involved or attached to the outcome of a situation, you can easily lose perspective. This is why the idea of being *egoless* is so important. If you find yourself taking things personally, quickly remind yourself that it's not about you, it's about the PBC.

Focus Is on the Process

Coaching provides great benefit to the PBC by helping him or her realize that he or she has all of the answers. Although both the coach and the PBC contribute special knowledge, experience, and insights to the coaching conversation, the PBC brings personal needs, perceptions, expectations, and firsthand knowledge of the job or situation to the table. The PBC ultimately knows the most about *how* best to do the work and what needs to occur. Coaches may bring experience, knowledge, and clarity about the topic being discussed, but most of all, coaches bring knowledge and skill of effective coaching techniques. Coaching is a process designed to make the most of what both people know: The coach knows the coaching process, while the PBC knows *what* needs to happen and *how* to make it happen (even if he or she doesn't realize it yet). The coach knows how to use the model and skills to draw these things out of the PBC.

Be aware of whether you are moving to the "fix" too quickly. Instead, your new focus for the coaching conversation is to be patient and follow a defined coaching process using clearly defined coaching skills and tailoring your approach to the needs of the PBC. The coaching process is the focus of the upcoming chapters.

Focus Is on the Gap

All coaching conversations have a purpose and direction, moving the PBC from a current reality to an ideal state. Coaching describes only the difference between what "is" and what is "desired to be." The coach's role is to assist the PBC in identifying what things look like now, compared to what they should look like (that is, what is the ideal or, in some cases, the best that can be hoped for?) and to identify the gap between. Once the PBC knows what the gap is, then you can draw out of the person *how* to close it. Because knowing where you are going is the first step to getting there.

Focus Is on the Future

Coaching should always be focused on what can change, that is, the future. Future-focus means people learn from the past, but cannot alter it. The coach can help the PBC focus on things that can be improved, modified, and changed. You should always approach a coaching session with the expectation that performance and commitment will be better because of the session. The past should be used only to help others understand how to improve the future. For instance, patterns of behavior can be pointed out, but only if they are relevant to a current trend or action and will serve to move the PBC forward in his or her progress.

Know When NOT to Coach

By now it should be clear that the distinguishing factor between the roles of *manager, instructor, mentor* and that of *coach* is based on who owns the *what* and the *how* of the interaction. There are, however, a few other roles that are commonly confused with coaching that are worthy of mentioning.

Coaching Is Not Counseling

Coaching is not counseling, and it is not a replacement for therapy. Why the distinction? In the last few years much controversy has been generated over the similarities between coaching and therapy. The debate became so heated that, at one point, one state even suggested requiring coaches to register as unlicensed therapists, a proposal that was met with great opposition from coaches and their professional organizations, because coaching is not therapy. This situation prompted most coaches and coaching websites to provide some manner of explanation between the two so that potential clients understand the differences.

Because both professions are relationship-based, and because coaching can get personal, it does make it more difficult to draw clear lines of distinction between each (thus the controversy). The best answer we can provide to explain the difference is that in many (not all) cases people go to a therapist to find out the *"why"* of something—"Why did this happen?" "Why do I feel this way?" "Why can't I stop X behavior?" And coaching is looking for the *"what"* and the *"how"* of getting the life you want—"What do I want out of life?" "What can I do to increase sales?" "How do I change careers?" "How do I change others' perceptions of my leadership style?" In general, coaches work with people whose issues, concerns, and problems are not psychologically debilitating. They do not work with clients on issues of or related to substance abuse, depression, emotional or physical abuse, anger management or psychoses. If a coach identifies a therapy issue, his or her role is to make a referral to a licensed mental health care professional or employee assistance program. Inside organizations, getting human resources involved is always a good idea. Is it possible for a person to work with a coach and have a therapist simultaneously? Absolutely, as long as the roles of coach and therapist remain distinctly separate.

If, after reading these paragraphs, you are still searching for the right answer to make the distinction between coaching and therapy, we encourage you to visit a few of the many coaching websites out there to read the multitude of different definitions provided by other coaches. Among these, the most thorough research was undoubtedly conducted by a research and development team put together by Thomas Leonard (1955–2003), founder of Coach University and Coachville, a man who is often credited with being the father of the coaching profession. His team comprised of therapists and coaches put together a very impressive comparison chart that weighs personal coaching against conventional therapy. You can view or download a copy of it at www.coachville.com/rd/020102therapypdf.pdf.

In the coaching versus therapy debate, Leonard said it best: "They are different ways of working, each with its own special value."

Coaching Is Not Consulting

Consulting, without a doubt, has its place in the business world today. Consultants and the services they provide are necessary and effective in specific business cases. Yet, one tragic trend occurring in the past few years is that many consultants, who have not received any training specific to coaching, have dubbed themselves "coaches." Please do not confuse consulting with coaching.

The most skilled coaches, even in the business world, have received schooling specific to the coaching field. They are either members of highly recognized and revered professional coaching organizations or and may have obtained (or are working toward) one of a variety of certifications offered from accredited coaching organizations such as the International Coach Federation (ICF) or the International Association of Coaches (IAC).

Certification is not a requirement, but highly skilled coaches certainly will have learned how to conduct coaching conversations using a coaching model, and they have honed specific coaching skills that allow the PBC to be the expert in engineering their own processes, solutions, and action plans.

Consultants, on the other hand, are experts in their fields who are brought in to provide insight and advice. Their focus and intent is to *solve* and to *tell*, not to coach. Consultants are sought out for their knowledge and are expected to make a difference by assessing a situation, dissecting it, sharing their knowledge and solutions about how to fix it or move forward, and assisting with a plan to implement such solutions. Typically, once consultants understand the situation, they offer and *direct* actions, solutions, and strategies. Simply stated, they provide both the *what* and the *how*, very similar to the *instructor role*.

With proper training and practice, many consultants make excellent coaches. Without it, chances are they will remain in the *instructor* role, being more directive, doing most of the talking and solving. This service is valuable. But its not coaching. If you are a consultant reading this book with a desire to learn coaching techniques and skills, we commend you and encourage you to read on.

Coaching for Commitment Is Not Sports Coaching

It is difficult to clearly differentiate sports coaching from the roles of *manager*, *instructor*, and *mentor* because most sports coaches use these roles regularly, even though their field is called coaching. Even though sports coaches have the title of "coach," it does not mean that they play the *coach role* (at least not exclusively) as defined by Coaching for Commitment and professional coaching organizations.

The distinction between sports coaches and the Coaching for Commitment variety is complicated further by the fact that different sports have different levels, layers, and types of coaches. An Olympic hopeful may only have one coach, while professional sports teams have many coaches. For example, football teams have head coaches that we would say are most closely aligned with the role of *manager;* the one who provides *what* needs to happen. Then there are the offensive and defensive coordinators, who provide both *what* needs to happen and *how* it should happen (instructor role) to either the players or the next level of coaches, and so on. When players seek advice on *how* to make something happen, they are seeking a mentor (*mentor role*) who can provide the specifics. So, even though they are all labeled coaches by profession, they play just as much of the *manager, instructor,* and *mentor* roles as does a business manager. Sports coaching and Coaching for Commitment are only similar when the coach does not dictate *what* needs to happen and *how* to make it happen and instead allows the athlete or team complete autonomy to make these decisions on their own.

Pretending to Coach

This chapter puts a lot of emphasis on distinguishing the various roles and helping you determine when you are coaching and what you should be doing while in the *coach role.*

Now that you know what coaching is and when to use it, use caution so that you don't coach everything and don't pretend to be coaching when you're not. This is dangerous territory. If you want to maintain ownership of either the *what* or the *how*, it's okay, just don't call what you are doing coaching. Know that you are using a different role and call it what it is (*manager, mentor, or instructor*).

The following are some examples of pretending to coach:

- Remember, if you are trying to lead the PBC to your solutions, you are not coaching.
  - If there is a solution you want the PBC to get to (namely yours) and you aren't willing or able to hear his or her ideas, don't coach the person, tell him or her instead.

- If there is an impact that you want the PBC to be aware of, tell him or her, rather than asking, because the PBC won't have the response you are looking for—especially if it is a situation in which the behavior is a performance-related issue.

  - For example: If the PBC's workplace behavior is having a negative impact on you or others, don't expect that by asking a question like, "How do you think your teammates felt when you . . .?" that the PBC will give the answer you are looking for. Instead, make a clear and direct statement about the impact of the behavior on the team.

- If the situation is a matter of legal or compliance concern–don't coach! Compliance or legal matters usually require one of the other roles—*manager, instructor,* or *mentor*—because people must know *what* they need to do or *how* to do it to remain compliant.

Every day, we witness coaches who try to drive conversations around to their way of thinking. One pitfall coaches fall into is starting a question with the words "Have you thought of . . .?" or asking closed-ended questions that only allow for one-word answers. Both of these suggest that the coach is trying to lead the PBC to his or her way of thinking. It is possible to do this without realizing it, so *be aware*.

If you have a specific answer you want to hear from the PBC, don't coach; use the *instructor role* and tell instead. Any scenario in which the PBC is expected to have the right answer (yours), read your mind or your needs without having the proper introduction, or conform to your biases is not coaching.

The following is an example of a manager who is pretending to coach:

COACH/CASEY: "Samir, I asked you to come and talk to me today because I want to discuss yesterday's team meeting."

PBC/SAMIR: "Sure, Casey, what's up?"

COACH/CASEY: "Did anything happen in yesterday's meeting that stands out to you?"

PBC/SAMIR: "I can't think of anything."

COACH/CASEY: "Samir, are you sure that you didn't do something that could have been considered inappropriate in yesterday's meeting?"

PBC/SAMIR: "I don't know, did I?"

COACH/CASEY: "Actually, you did. You put Rose down in front of the entire team. Do you realize how that kind of behavior affects the rest of the team?"

PBC/SAMIR: "I'm not sure what I said, but I'm sure I was just kidding. . . ."

COACH/CASEY: "Samir, you are an important member of this team and I can't help you if you don't let me. What can we do to make it so you understand the impact that your comments have on your team members?"

PBC/SAMIR (Joking): "Well, Casey, I could not come to the team meeting. . . ."

In a discussion with Casey, we found out that she did not want to come across too harshly in her talk with Samir, but wanted him to own up to what had happened in the team meeting without her having to point it out. She wanted him to see the error of his ways, apologize for the behavior, and swear to never do it again. Unfortunately, Samir is seeing things from a different perspective and believes he didn't do anything but make a joke to another team member. It was of such little impact to him that he didn't even remember what he said. If she had been in the *coach role* instead of the *manager role*, it would be Casey's job to state the observed behavior to Samir, along with the impact of this behavior. (*Why* are we having this conversation?) Then, once Samir recognized and agreed that the incident had occurred, Casey would ask questions to get him to come up with ideas on *what* to do differently next time, and *how* to make his behavior changes a reality. In doing so she would gain his input as well as his commitment. Instead, this coach was pretending to coach.

Simply Uncoachable

Just as you should not pretend to coach when the situation does not necessitate using the *coach role*, you should be aware of the opposite scenario, one in which the situation necessitates the *coach role*, yet the PBC is not coachable.

A good question, and one that should be answered *before* entering the coaching conversation, is, "Is the PBCcoachable?" Typically, people are coachable. Although the truly uncoachable are out there.

Few though they may be, there are clues to identifying the simply uncoachable. The following list of simply uncoachable traits can be used to determine whether your potential PBC is a tough nut (coachable) or a lost cause (uncoachable). These are extreme traits, and typically, more than one of them needs to be present for someone to be deemed uncoachable:

- Constantly blames others, processes, procedures, or the environment for poor performance or behavior.
- Never takes personal accountability.
- Never takes on additional responsibilities.
- Rarely accomplishes assigned duties.
- Is always defensive.
- Is constantly angry and resentful.
- Always plays the victim role.
- Repeatedly refuses to be coached or says that he or she is not interested in coaching or development planning.
- Refuses to participate in the performance review process.
- Constantly creates problems within the team.
- Is always combative.
- Is constantly disruptive.
- Is consistently uncommunicative.
- Doesn't respect his or her colleagues or you.

- Consistently asks for feedback, yet regularly retaliates when it is given.

- Consistently calls off or is absent from work.

- Has a diminished mental capacity to reason and process information or has a medical condition that would render him or her otherwise unable to reason or process information or cannot be held accountable for his or her actions.

If you are dealing with someone who is uncoachable and you have tried your best, depending on the severity of the situation, here are a few options for you to consider:

- Rather than continuing to try to coach, play a stronger *manager role* whenever dealing with this person. Tell this person *what* you expect. You may even want to use the *instructor role* and tell *what* you expect and *how* it should be accomplished. Either of these roles require you to be more directive in your approach. Tell more than ask or make assignments instead of asking for actions.

- If you think the person is a tough nut, versus a lost cause, take accountability for the coaching relationship and seriously look at the level of trust that exists between you and the PBC. If there is no trust, coaching will not work. Ask yourself whether you have contributed in any way to the PBC being uncoachable? Have you fully made the shift to the *coach role* when interacting? Have you been controlling the *what* or the *how* or interjecting your prejudices, biases, or personal values into the conversation? Remember, when playing the *coach role*, remain *egoless*, release control of the *what* and the *how*, and ensure that a high level of trust exists between you and the PBC.

- If you have reason to believe the person is not coachable due to highly personal or mental health reasons, be prepared to suggest an employee assistance program, a therapist, or legal counsel if warranted. Have your referral resources ready. In addition, do not hesitate to contact one of these resources if you are not sure how to handle the situation, and document, document, document.

- When dealing with human resource issues, strive to be *egoless* and remain objective, keeping your emotions and tone in check. Observe and document inappropriate behaviors and actions. I involve your HR representative early. They are highly skilled individuals who are trained to deal with such matters.

- If someone is resistant but coachable, you may want to hire an external coach to work with the person. Sometimes a new coach brings new perspectives and can be perceived as more objective or neutral. An external coach is not tied to internal politics, and this can be good. Exercise caution here because the last thing you want to do is only bring in external coaches to "fix" people. This is counterproductive to the Coaching for Commitment Culture you are trying to create. (If you plan to use external coaches, the general rule is to use them for your top performers as often as for your difficult ones.) When hiring an external coach, take the following steps with the PBC first:

  - Confront the person's behavior.

  - Address the impacts of the person's behavior. What is the impact it is having on others, that person (tap into the intrinsic motivators), and the company?

  - Share the concept of coaching and its benefits. Talk about what coaching is and what it can do and why a neutral party may be better suited to working with the person.

  - Create an agenda for what the person will work on with the coach. Either find a way to create a shared agenda about what should be worked on with a coach or be willing to let the potential PBC choose his or her own agenda. Feel free to set terms such as the person can create his or her own agenda if it is based on 360-degree feedback, etc.

- Get the person involved in selecting the right coach. If you want results, don't pick a coach for the person. Let the potential PBC interview at least three coaches and then make a selection. This will ensure a better fit and better results.

- Agree on how feedback or updates will be communicated back to you and other stakeholders. Your mutual feedback methodology should ensure coaching conversations between coach and PBC are totally confidential, while providing you with adequate information to note progress. Usually, the PBC is tasked with providing regular and honest progress reports to the manager. (Many coaches will not provide progress reports to stakeholders unless otherwise designated in a coaching contract, and even then, disclosure of conversation content is not included.)

Coaching is not about being the hero or the one who can fix everything. Coaching is an art that takes learning and practice to be successful. Coaching occurs when you make the mental shift to coach and you are conscious of the fact that you are coaching. The remainder of this book will focus exclusively on the *coach role*. It will provide you with a coaching process, model, and skills and explain how to plan and prepare for your coaching conversations. As you make the shift to the *coach* role, use these processes and techniques as your guide.

Please note that Chapter 7, Plan to Coach, provides additional tips, tools, and resources for enhancing your performance when in the *coach role*. It includes detailed information on coaching channels, tools, worksheets for note-taking, as well as suggestions for conducting performance coaching conversations.

Coaching Moment

If you have not done so already, complete the Coaching Skills Inventory (CSI)—available separately from Pfeiffer—to determine which role you gravitate toward and your coaching gap.

Current Reality: If you have taken the CSI, what role do you gravitate toward most often? If you haven't taken the CSI, based on reading this chapter, what role do you think you gravitate toward most often?

Think about how much time you spend in each role. Enter your answers below so that the percentages equal 100.

Coach   _____ percent
Manager   _____ percent
Instructor   _____ percent
Mentor   _____ percent

How conscious are you about what role you are operating from when dealing with people (*coach, manager, instructor*, and *mentor*)?

Ideal State: What will it take for you to make the shift to the *coach role*?

Action Plan: Identify one or two things you want to work on from this chapter so that you can make a conscious shift to the *coach role* and solicit all answers from the PBC. What is one way you can set aside biases in dealing with others? What is one thing you can do to be more *egoless* in your interactions?

Chapter Summary

The *coach role* can best be distinguished from *manager, instructor,* and *mentor* by who owns the *what* and the *how* components of the interaction.

- Managers own the *what*, not the *how*.
- Instructors own both the *what* and the *how*.
- Mentors own the *how*, not the *what*.
- Coaches own neither the *what* nor the *how*. These are owned by the PBC!

All four roles have their place and provide value based on the type and needs of the conversation at hand. The goal is not to eliminate any of these roles or even lessen them, but rather to increase your awareness of the shift that needs to occur as you transition from *manager*, *instructor*, or m*entor* into the *coach role*.

When to Coach

The *coach role* is best used for interactions that move the PBC forward using all of his or her ideas and solutions. The coach's role is to help the PBCs gain insight and understanding regarding the topic of conversation, not to solve problems for him or her.

- 80 percent of a coach's time is spent listening.
- 20 percent is asking mostly open-ended *coaching questions*.

Shift Happens

Making the mental shift to the *coach role* requires that you

- Let go of both the *what* and the *how*,
- Eliminate biases and prejudices,
- Become *egoless*, and
- Clear the clutter.

Who Should Coach

Coaching is for anyone who has a desire to help others succeed and for those who possess the knowledge and skills that it takes to work through the process of a coaching conversation, using the Coaching for Commitment approach.

Benefits of Coaching

- The value proposition for coaching is impressive.
- Coaching strengthens work relationships and creates high-performing individuals and teams.

Perspectives of a Coach

- Focus is on the PBC.
- Focus is on the process.
- Focus is on the gap.
- Focus is on the future.

Know When NOT to Coach

- Coaching is not counseling.
- Coaching is not consulting.
- Coaching for Commitment is not sports coaching.

Pretending to Coach

Don't coach everything and don't pretend to be coaching when you're not. If you want to maintain ownership of either the *what* or the *how*, use the appropriate role, and don't call what you are doing coaching.

Simply Uncoachable

Know whether the PBC is coachable. Typically, most people are coachable, although the truly uncoachable are out there.

- Instead, use a different role, most commonly that of *manager* or *instructor*.
- Take accountability for your part in the coaching relationship. Did you make the shift and were you *egoless*?
- Have your referral sources ready.
- Involve Human Resources.
- Document, Document, Document!

CHAPTER 3

The Coaching Process

"Coaching is a process, not an event!"

—Cindy Coe

SUCCESSFUL COACHING follows a logical sequence or flow and requires the use of specific coaching skills and techniques.

If you mean to *control* rather than trust the natural flow and content of a coaching conversation, you may be disappointed, because these conversations are with people who also have some need to control their own outcomes. Skillful coaches are disciplined. They do not do or say whatever comes to mind. Instead, they do and say what furthers the process of coaching toward successful outcomes.

Undisciplined conversations, in contrast to coaching conversations, do not follow a specific process and model and do not employ the intentional use of prescribed skills. A common example of an undisciplined conversation is the ease with which you may start solving problems before you have developed sufficient information to even understand the real problem or its root cause. Another example is the tendency to give information about some action or procedure that is not helpful because the information is redundant or irrelevant to the other person's needs.

Desired outcomes occur most consistently in coaching when you concentrate on following a purposeful process, rather than when you concentrate on controlling the content of the coaching conversation.

From here on, we will focus on the *coach role* exclusively, which is represented by the bottom half of the illustration (Figure 3.1) that was initially presented in Chapter 2.

Figure 3.1. Role Model

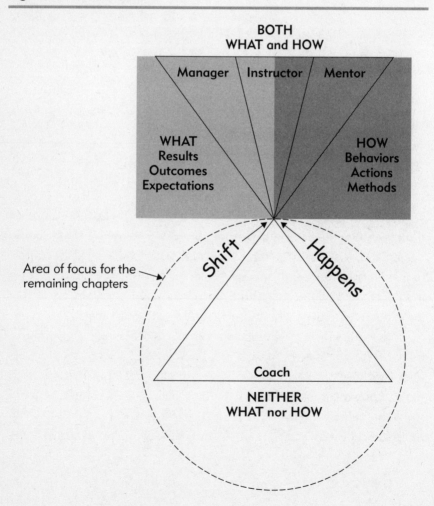

Before moving on, we want to briefly mention that coaching conversations can occur using a variety of methods or coaching channels:

- Face-to-Face
- Virtual:
  - Phone/Teleconference
  - Email
  - Video/Web Conference

These channels, which are discussed in greater detail in Chapter 7, are relevant because effective coaching conversations can happen using any of these channels. This means that the information you will learn in this and all subsequent chapters can be used with any of the coaching channels.

Coaching Prism

Part of making the *shift* to the *coach role* is about following a defined coaching process, which includes the use of a coaching model and clearly defined coaching skills. The coaching *process* is represented by the Coaching Prism (see Figure 3.2).

Figure 3.2. Coaching Prism

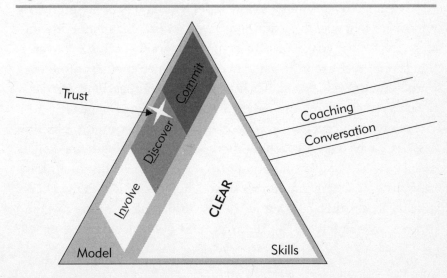

When the elements defined in the Coaching Prism are applied to your coaching conversations, you will be well on your way to becoming a skillful coach.

Before we get into the four elements of the Coaching Prism, it is helpful to recall how a prism works. A single ray of light enters one side of a prism, the components of the prism refract the light, and it comes out on the other side as a brilliant display of rainbow-colored light. The complexity of the Coaching Prism is similar in nature to any prism. The white light is Trust, and the rainbow is the coaching conversation. The components in between are the InDiCom coaching model and CLEAR coaching skills.

Trust

Without light, the rainbow of colors will not appear from the other side of the prism. Similarly, without trust, there is no coaching conversation. Trust is the primary catalyst and main ingredient of all coaching conversations. Mutual trust between you and the PBC must be established and maintained throughout the coaching process. Trust is the basis for making the entire coaching conversation possible. Chapter 4 is devoted to the coach's role in establishing and maintaining a relationship that is based on trust.

The InDiCom Coaching Model

All coaching conversations follow a defined model, although it may not appear that way to the untrained eye. A coaching model provides structure for the coaching conversation. A good coaching conversation should feel like a casual conversation, even though it follows a purposeful process. No matter how long or short coaching conversations are, be conscious and move through the defined stages.

Following a coaching model is essential to becoming a skillful coach. Coaches use a coaching model and follow the defined steps as they assist the PBC in moving from a current reality to an ideal state. The coaching model presented here is called the *InDiCom coaching model*. InDiCom stands for the three phases of the coaching process: *In* = Involve; *Di* = Discover; and *Com* = Commit. You will have the opportunity to learn the InDiCom coaching model in detail in Chapter 5.

CLEAR Coaching Skills

As the light of trust continues to move through the Coaching Prism, the next coaching component, used with all phases of the InDiCom coaching model, are the CLEAR coaching skills. These skills are very specific to the *coach role*. Although many of the coaching skills that you learn may be familiar to you, because you use them in everyday conversations, you will learn how to apply these common communication skills from a coach perspective to achieve maximum impact in a coaching conversation and to be conscious of your use of them. The skills are Challenge, Listen, Encourage, Ask, and Refine. As you apply them to your coaching conversations, they become the CLEAR coaching skills.

Some skills may be easier for you to implement than others. Integrating all the skills into your coaching conversation takes sustained effort, time, and practice. Chapter 6 is devoted to the CLEAR coaching skills.

The Coaching Conversation

This is where it all comes together. You will learn how to apply the components of the Coaching Prism—Trust, InDiCom coaching model, and CLEAR coaching skills—to conduct a coaching conversation. Coaching conversations are mutual interactions that should feel natural. That is what makes coaching an art. It may look simple to the untrained eye, yet so many things are working together to make it happen. Chapter 8 is devoted to the coaching conversation and provides sample conversations for reference.

Putting the Pieces Together

For some, it is helpful to be able to see the big picture. Figure 3.3 illustrates how all the pieces discussed so far fit together. Note how the Coaching Prism fits easily into the *coach role* triangle at the bottom of the *Role Model*.

Figure 3.3. The Big Picture

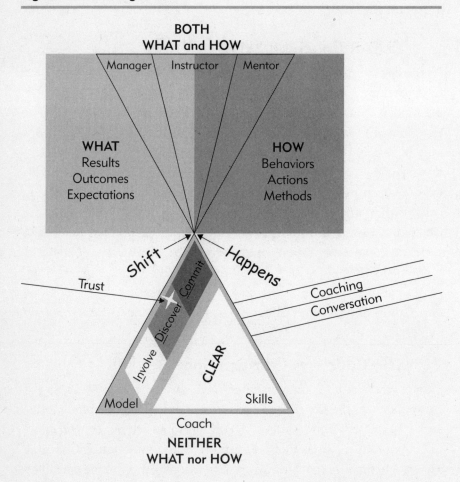

The Coaching Prism may appear complex, but complex does not mean impossible. Complex can mean rich and amazing results, especially if you are willing to strive to do your best and open your mind to coaching possibilities.

Coaching Moment

Current Reality: Based on what you have learned so far, how often do you coach using a purposeful process? Use a rating scale of 1 to 10 (1 = Never and 10 = Every time I coach).

Ideal State: Where do you want to be on this scale?

Action Plan: What is one thing you can do to close the gap and adopt a coaching process?

Chapter Summary

This chapter defined the coaching process, which is represented by the Coaching Prism.

There are four components to the Coaching Prism:

- Trust
- InDiCom coaching model
- CLEAR coaching skills
- Coaching conversation

These four components are depicted by a Coaching Prism. Trust is the light that enters the prism, while the InDiCom coaching model and CLEAR coaching skills make up the technical components inside the prism. When used in combination, these elements generate a colorful and *brilliant* spectrum: the coaching conversation.

4

Trust

"You can't shake hands with a clenched fist."

—Indira Gandhi

TRUST is the first component of the coaching process. It allows you to achieve superior performance as a coach and long-term commitment and action from the PBC. Trust is the light that enters the Coaching Prism (Figure 4.1). It makes the coaching conversation possible. Trust is building relationships with others.

Often, trust is a core issue when communication breaks down between people. People don't trust themselves or don't trust others. That is why it is so very important that you build trust before your coaching conversations begin and maintain it throughout. Trust is the most important aspect of coaching because every effective coaching relationship is built on a solid trust foundation.

Establishing and Maintaining Trust

In Chapter 2, The Coach Role, coaching biases and being *egoless* were discussed as a part of the mental shift that is required to move from one of the other roles (*manager, mentor, instructor*) into the *coach role*. Simply put, leaving biases aside and becoming *egoless* is a precursor to

Figure 4.1. Coaching Prism

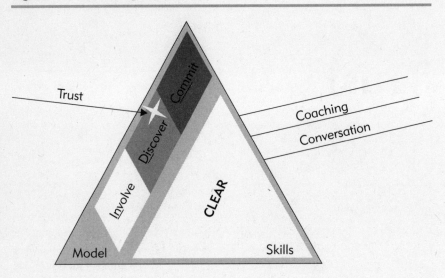

building trust with others. Trust is about relationships. So is coaching. By being open to the needs of the person being coached (PBC), you indicate that you are ready to trust and be trusted by others.

Trust is one of those things that takes time and energy to build and only moments to destroy. Establishing and maintaining trust requires sustained, conscious effort on the part of the coach.

Trust adds the humanistic component to the coaching conversation. It assumes that the coach has genuine concern for the PBC, whether it is concern in wanting the person to succeed or concern for him or her as a person. It also assumes that the coach is comfortable in his or her own skin and operates from a place of genuineness instead of superficiality.

Building and maintaining trust means that you are honest, authentic, take accountability for your actions and behaviors, and demonstrate respect for others.

Being Honest

Be honest! Noel Coward once said, "It is discouraging how many people are shocked by honesty and how few [are shocked] by deceit."

Often it seems that the brand of honesty that is used in personal interactions with others (especially in the workplace) has become more about varying levels of deceit—numbers, political correctness, jockeying for position, ulterior motives—than about honesty. To build trust, you cannot have ulterior motives.

Being honest sometimes means being direct, in a respectful way, and not avoiding the tough stuff. Be supportive in your intent and share what can sometimes be difficult truths in order to affect a positive change. Our motto is, "Say what you mean but don't say it mean; how the other person takes it is up to him or her!"

Being Authentic

Being authentic means that you are genuine and honest in your dealings with others. It means you are comfortable with being human in front of others and that you make an effort to "have your own house in order" so to speak. Having your house in order assumes that you have dealt with or are dealing with any of your own personal or professional issues separately and, above all, that you don't transfer your fears, insecurities, frustrations, or other issues to others when in the *coach role*. Being authentic suggests your willingness to give and take in getting to know people on a more personal level and, above all, not being hypocritical.

Because coaching encourages the PBC to act from a place of authenticity, it stands to reason that the coach needs to operate from a place of authenticity as well—one that is based on feelings, emotions, carefully weighing the impact of actions, exploring obstacles, and in many cases accepting or managing the perceptions of others, even when you may not agree with them.

Being Accountable

You are 100 percent accountable for 50 percent of the relationship. Take responsibility for what you need to, and empower the PBC to do the same.

Whether you realize it or not, you influence every coaching conversation—and you do so for better or worse. Most often, coaching does not fail because the PBC is poorly endowed or poorly motivated. It fails because of poorly trained, poorly disciplined, and inauthentic coaches. Take accountability for your part when you need to and hold the PBC accountable for his or hers!

What does this mean for you? For starters it means that as a coach you don't place blame. Nor do you allow the PBC to blame others for his or her lack of performance or detrimental behaviors. Blaming fosters a victim mentality. It creates a lack of responsibility and personal accountability, meaning that the person (coach or PBC) does not have to take responsibility for his or her actions or for improving performance. Blaming sets the coach and PBC up for a battle of wills—a mental competition. This is counter-productive to coaching. (See blame examples in the *Disrespectful Behavior* section of this chapter.)

Being Respectful

Being respectful means that you want the PBC to improve and believe that he or she can do so. Avoid any behavior that encourages the PBC to become defensive, to feel guilty, or to lose confidence. The purpose of coaching is *not* to help the PBC feel worse or to despair over incompetence. The purpose is to find very individualized ways for the PBC to be a superior performer. When you coach, you must never lose sight of what you are trying to achieve—positive change and commitment to sustained, superior performance. Check your ego and your agenda (especially if it is hidden) at the door. We can't stress this enough. Coaching is not a win/lose venture.

Being respectful also means that you behave in such a way to stimulate a free and open development of information and do nothing to inhibit its flow. It is being courteous, professional, and polite to others. Using respectful behaviors builds and maintains trust.

It is easy to become confused about respect. People who have attended our coaching workshops sometimes ask, "How am I supposed to treat someone who isn't worthy of my respect?" Or they ask, "How am I supposed to respond to something that I know is just an excuse?" or "How can I pretend that people are doing a good job when I know they aren't?"

These questions suggest a common confusion about respect. All too commonly people think of respect as something that people *earn* or as a treatment that is given to only those who *deserve it*. Respect during a coaching conversation is a characteristic that helps the conversation work. It should be automatic and, when it's present, coaching conversations are much more successful.

People feel respected to the degree that they have been encouraged to contribute information and ideas. In contrast, disrespectful behaviors elicit useless information, promote sarcasm, and hinder development. Disrespectful behavior can destroy or undermine trust in seconds. In a coaching conversation it serves no good purpose to stimulate resistance, to foster resentment, to promote emotional detachment, or to block the sharing of information—all of which are likely to occur when a coach does not communicate respect.

Think about what happens when you do not feel respected by another person in a conversation. This occurs when the other person does not listen, interrupts, and discounts the value of your ideas or uses sarcasm inappropriately. What is going on when others behave this way is that they are not encouraging you to participate fully in the mutual development of information. When respect is not present, the coaching conversation will inevitably fail.

Respectful Behaviors

Coaches who are respectful in their behaviors toward others communicate respect through statements that contribute to positive self-regard and building a trusting relationship. Examples of respectful behavior and statements are provided below.

Make a PBC feel like he or she is the most important person at that moment and acknowledge that the problem or issues are real, at least to him or her. The following statements show that you value individualization and uniqueness:

- "I can tell this is really upsetting to you and seems to be heavy on your mind."

- "You have really given this a lot of thought."
- "I want you to know that others recognize your challenges."
- "From your perspective, it must seem like there's no end in sight."

Boost self-esteem by making people feel good about themselves, proud of who they are and what they say and do.

- "That was a brilliant idea!"
- "You should be proud of yourself for that."
- "I'm so impressed with what you just said."
- "You've mastered a lot since our last conversation!"
- "You always know how to figure these things out!"

When you don't place blame, try to find blame, or question someone's intentions, you are assuming both innocence and positive intent.

- "Since you can't undo the situation, let's focus on what you can do."
- "I need to ask a few questions because I need help putting all of the pieces together, not because I'm questioning what you did."
- "This is not about finding fault; let's focus instead on how to fix things."
- "I'm sure you did everything you could. Where do you go from here?"
- "What do you think might help you to get to work on time?"
- "I need that report. When can you have it ready?"

When you believe that it *"is all about the person being coached* (PBC)," that is the beginning of building trust. Respect means that you make people feel like they are trusted individuals and that they can trust you.

- "You can tell me anything."
- "Our coaching conversation today will be all about you."

- "I appreciate you taking me into your confidence. How can I help?"

- "I hope you will trust me. I'm here to help."

- "What would you like to talk about today?"

Consistently create and honor respect in your coaching conversations. Learn to use behaviors that encourage a free exchange of opinions and information. Learn to avoid behaviors that invite resistance or resentment and that block the exchange of information, ideas, and trust: behaviors that are disrespectful.

Disrespectful Behaviors

Coaches who are disrespectful in their behaviors toward others communicate disrespect through statements that whittle away at positive self-regard and diminish trusting relationships. Regardless of its mainstream popularity on television sit-coms, and in everyday life, sarcasm is counter-productive to the trust relationship. Examples of disrespectful behavior and statements are provided below.

People feel discounted when you treat them like they are not individuals either by making them part of a larger whole where everyone thinks, feels, and behaves the same, or expecting them to be just like everyone else. Making sweeping generalizations also makes people feel discounted.

- "You are always late."

- "Don't you think you are overreacting just a little?"

- "Join the club; everyone has the same problem."

- "You are overreacting."

- "The problem is not as big as you make it."

- "It can't be that bad."

- "Don't make a mountain out of a mole hill."

- "Everyone else seems to get along just fine. Why don't you get with the program?"

Ridiculing is the act of saying things that exaggerate another person's mistakes to make an example of him or her, pointing out failures for sport or to improve your own self-worth, making fun of another person, or making comments at someone else's expense simply because you can.

- "Congratulations, Bob, I can only conclude from your behavior yesterday that you intended to find the most creative way possible to make the whole team look like fools in front of the vice president."
- "I know you don't believe in dressing for success, but must you always look like an unmade bed?"
- "That was the most idiotic thing I've ever heard."
- "I thought you were smarter than that!"
- "You really disappointed me by not turning in your report on time."
- "You're still making the same mistakes we covered last time."
- "Duh!" or "whatever!"

If you have a hidden agenda and sidetrack the conversation by encouraging the PBC to provide information that is immaterial to the root cause, just to serve your purposes, you are being irrelevant.

- "Before we get started, tell me about your new manager. I heard he's really old school."
- "How long did you think about this problem and who else did you talk to before you decided to come to me?"
- "What did your boss say?"
- "While you were there, did you overhear anything new about the project?"
- "Did she happen to share anything with you about me?"

Blame calls the intentions and truths of others into question.

- "Did you do this?"
- "I don't think you've tried hard enough to get along with them."
- "You're misunderstanding what's going on."
- "If it's not your fault, whose is it?"
- "Who was responsible for the breakdown?"

Gestures made during face-to-face interactions and verbal nuances during virtual interactions can sometimes communicate disrespect.

- Rolling eyes.
- Heavy sighing.
- Stoic or stern looks.
- Verbal "tsk."
- Waving off someone with your hand.

Using disrespectful behaviors may not dissolve trust immediately. Blame and sarcasm erode trust over a period of time. Either way, the damage done is difficult to repair and takes valuable time and energy. It is also important to recognize that use of tone can often be the determining factor as to whether a comment or gesture is respectful or disrespectful. How can you be aware of your language, gestures, and tone in order to convey the utmost respect to others?

In creating a trust relationship, make a connection on a personal level with the persons you coach. You should know something about the PBC's interests. What's important to the PBC? What is a passion or a motivator for him or her? If the coaching relationship is new, before you jump right into a coaching conversation, make some small talk that doesn't have anything to do with work concerns or problems. Find out what the PBC is passionate about. What charities does he or she support or offer time to? Ask how the family is or what happened over the weekend. In other words, express a genuine interest in who they are, not just in what they do.

Coaching Moment

Current Reality: How much do you trust your clients, the people who work with/for you, and your partners? How much do you think they trust you? What behaviors or actions let you know this? Think of a person you coach regularly. What is the level of trust that exists between you and the PBC?

You can assess the extent to which a trusting relationship exists by measuring the degree of influence that the PBC has during coaching conversations. This level can be determined by assessing the following statements, where Always = 5 and Not at All = 1:

	Always				**Not at all**
1. I avoid using disrespectful tones, gestures, and sarcasm with the PBC.	5	4	3	2	1
2. I am honest in sharing my observations, not opinions, with the PBC.	5	4	3	2	1
3. I am respectful when I communicate with the PBC.	5	4	3	2	1
4. I encourage the PBC to take genuine ownership of the situation or problem and accountability for moving forward.	5	4	3	2	1
5. I take accountability for my part in issues with the PBC.	5	4	3	2	1
6. I am authentic and do not transfer my "baggage," insecurities, or issues to the PBC.	5	4	3	2	1

Ideal State: The higher your score, the better the trust relationship. What really matters is the PBC's perception of the level of trust that exists. Would the PBC agree with your answers?

Action Plan: How will you close the gap between the level of trust you believe exists and the PBC's perception? What would you like the trust relationship to be/look/feel like with each person you thought of? What is one way you can take personal accountability and improve trust in your relationships with others?

Extra Credit: Think about one person whom you struggle with on a regular basis. Assess the level of trust you believe the relationship to have. What is your role in building trust? Create an action plan for addressing the gap.

Chapter Summary

Trust is critical to coaching; it is the light that makes the coaching conversation possible.

In order to establish and maintain trust, a coach must be honest, authentic, respectful, and accountable when dealing with others. Avoid disrespectful behaviors, comments, and gestures that destroy or undermine trust.

CHAPTER 5

The InDiCom Coaching Model

"Vision without execution is merely hallucination."

—Steve Case

PEOPLE OFTEN have no way to analyze systematically what works and what does not work in coaching because they have no baseline or model against which they can compare what they do. Before coaches begin to learn that successful coaching follows a sequential model, most people think of their current "coaching conversations" as casual inputs or helpful guidance between the coach and the people they are trying to coach. Sometimes these conversations work, and sometimes they do not, but in the end if they do work, the coach often does not know what made it work.

Coaching that does not follow a proven model may sometimes succeed, but it will more often fail or have temporary results. Coaching conversations that have a random shape produce random results. Coaching does not fail, but those who do not discipline themselves to employ a specific model for coaching can set themselves up to fail when in the *coach role*.

Learning to use a coaching model like the one introduced in this chapter will ultimately transform the way you conduct coaching conversations. As you become more in tune with the PBC and the coaching conversation, you will be less mentally distracted by the need to solve. By using a model, you will become more creative and less reactive in your questions and responses.

The model presented in this chapter is universal in nature in that it can be used for *all* coaching interactions, from enhancing top performers who are already successful to addressing under-performers in need of improvement. The model can be used for short, quick coaching moments or for longer coaching conversations. It can be used when you want to help someone identify an issue that needs to be addressed and discover creative solutions to move forward, or when a person comes to you with a concern or situation he or she wants help with. It can be used one time or over a period of time.

Please note that for simplicity's sake and so that you can learn the basics of the model, this chapter largely discusses the use of the InDiCom Coaching Model in conversations during which the PBC approaches the coach; that is, the PBC brings the *why* to the coaching conversation (*Why* are we having this conversation?). The same model is used when the coach brings the *why* to the table, often called a performance coaching conversation, discussed further in Chapter 7. This chapter will help you to learn the basics of the model so that you have a solid foundation upon which to hone your performance coaching skills when you read Chapter 7.

The InDiCom coaching model is part of the Coaching Prism (see Figure 5.1 on the next page).

The model consists of three stages:

- Stage I: **In**volve
- Stage II: **Di**scover
- Stage III: **Com**mit

In succession, using the first few letters from each stage, the name InDiCom (pronounced: *In-dee-com*) Coaching Model emerges.

Figure 5.1. Coaching Prism

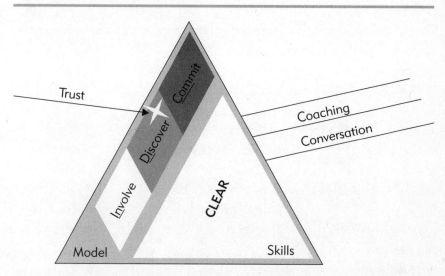

The three stages of the InDiCom coaching model (shown in Figure 5.2) flow into one another. Although the stages of the InDiCom coaching model appear linear in nature, they are not. The stages mark the transition from one set of goals to the next, and yet it is possible to move through one state only to return to it later. This is especially true of Stage 2, which can be repeated multiple times before the conversation is over. Moving back and forth between the stages is part of the process and is okay—as long as the overall flow of the conversation continually moves forward toward the ideal state.

Make it your goal to know the three stages of the model and their corresponding goals so well that they become second nature to you. The first time you read this chapter you will gain a good foundation for conducting a successful coaching conversation. Becoming a skillful coach takes time and practice. Reread this chapter as often as you need to in order to master the elements of the InDiCom coaching model. By rereading it, practicing the stages, and accomplishing the goals at each stage, you will discover a powerful coaching approach.

And remember, you must establish and maintain *trust* throughout all stages of the coaching model. It is the coach's role to ensure that the PBC

Figure 5.2. InDiCom Coaching Model

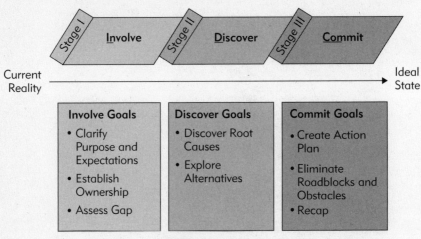

InDiCom Coaching Model

feels comfortable with you as the coach, that he or she can trust you with whatever information is shared, and that your coaching conversations are confidential, except in cases of legality or contractual arrangements (legally obligated to disclose by court order or coaching contract agreement that specifically states disclosure arrangements, that is, HR manager receives updates from the coach regarding the PBC). Also, the conversation needs to feel free and easy. Therefore, even though you, as the coach, are progressing through the stages of the InDiCom coaching model, the interaction should feel like a normal conversation. This is true for "coaching moments" as well—when you or the PBC wants to have a quick coaching conversation that only lasts a few minutes.

InDiCom Coaching Model
Stage I: Involve

The main goal of the Involve stage is to establish *why* the conversation is occurring. "*Why* are we having this conversation?" Typically, coaching conversations occur to resolve an issue, discuss a topic, address a performance issue, or gain insight. In determining *why*, seek to clarify the purpose of the conversation and determine expectations.

Each stage of the InDiCom coaching model has goals that you, the coach, will ensure are met in your coaching conversations before moving to the next stage. The goals that you should have in mind at the Involve stage are:

- Clarify the Purpose and Expectations
- Establish Ownership
- Assess the Gap

Clarify Purpose and Expectations

It is the coach's role to ensure that the purpose and expectations for the coaching conversation are clear. This means that the purpose and expectations are identified and communicated, either by the coach or the PBC. The purpose identifies the reason the coaching conversation is occurring while expectations are identified as outcomes, results, potential, or opportunity.

As mentioned, if the coach brings the *why* (*Why* are we having this conversation?) to the PBC, then this is likely a performance coaching conversation (Chapter 7). If the PBC brings the *why* to the coach, the coach's role is to listen to what the PBC wants to discuss and assist in clarifying and/or restating the issue. If the PBC brings a laundry list to the table enumerating multiple areas to focus on, you will ask questions that help the PBC determine which topic to focus on first. Similarly, if the PBC is not aware that that purpose includes a multitude of topics, you should help the PBC separate them out, and then let the PBC decide which one to focus on first.

PBC: "I know I'm my own worst critic and I'm really hard on myself, but my peers don't see me the way my employees see me and my boss sees me a totally different way, too."

COACH: "There appear to be a few different things going on here. Which would you like to focus on first: being your own worst critic and hard on yourself or how people perceive you differently? "

Sometimes it's as simple as the coach responding with one of the following questions:

- "What would you like to accomplish in our time together?"
- "What would you like to focus on?"
- "You mentioned more than one topic. Which one would you like to concentrate on today?"

The coach also needs to ensure that expectations are clear. Typically, this means that the coach assists the PBC to determine his or her expectations, desired outcomes, desired results, potential, or opportunity. By clarifying expectations, insight on the gap is obtained because the expectations usually help determine the desired or ideal state. The coach might ask:

- "How will you know when you have reached your ideal?"
- "What results would you like to see?"
- "What would you like to see as a result?"

Clarifying expectations also means that you may need to clarify constraints (such as time), confidentiality, roles, or responsibilities in the opening dialog of the coaching conversation. When it is appropriate or needed, affirm for the PBC that he or she can trust you and that your coaching conversation is confidential. Confirming confidentiality provides extra comfort to the PBC. You may also need to let the PBC know that you will not be solving the problem, but your role as a coach is to help him or her get to a solution. If there is a timeframe you are working within, confirm the amount of time you plan to spend with the PBC. Clarify things such as the coach's role, concerns about the coaching process, and follow-up sessions. For example:

- "I only have about fifteen minutes right now and I know how important this is to you. Let's get started and we can always schedule more time later if that works for you."

- "Coaching sessions typically last forty-five minutes with a follow-up session in one to two weeks. Will that work for you?"

- "This is your time. It's all about you. That means you can decide what we talk about, whether it's a challenge you're facing or something you're excited about. During this time I will be in the *coach role*. That means two things: one, what you share is completely confidential and, two, I won't solve things for you. Instead, I'll listen and ask you questions to help you figure out your own answers."

- "Thank you for trusting me as your coach. Everything that we share will remain confidential; in fact, I will not even disclose to anyone that I am your coach without your permission. If you would like to share any information we discuss, you are welcome to do so."

- "As your coach I'm here to help. Just know that I'm not going to solve this for you, but I will ask you some powerful questions that will lead you to discover your own creative solutions. This is all about you."

Establish Ownership

The coach's role is to help the PBC identify ownership regarding the issue. Typically, the coach does not own the problem or item of discussion and it must remain that way. That means that the coach should not be committing to doing the follow-up work or implementing the action plan. The PBC needs to own the situation, problem, or request and be responsible and accountable for making the agreed-on changes or progress. One way to avoid taking on too much ownership as the coach is to avoid the use of the word "we" and to use "you" instead (e.g. "What can you do . . .?").

When the PBC communicates the purpose of the coaching conversation, establishing ownership is much easier because the PBC is the one seeking assistance from the coach and already owns the topic.

Therefore, the PBC's ownership of the situation is implied. There are times, however, when you will have to help the PBC narrow the scope or refocus the conversation to keep it within the PBC's span of control or influence. To do this, the coach might ask:

- "I know you dislike the way he manages his people and you'd like for him to change, but this is about you. What is your role in the situation?"

- "I realize the other team members can sometimes do things you don't like. What is your part in making the situation better?"

Assess the Gap

During the Involve stage, focus on assessing the gap and having the PBC take ownership for his or her role in closing the gap. The PBC should be able to identify where he or she is and where he or she wants to be.

It is the PBC's responsibility to own the gap and identify what the ideal or end state should look like, including actions and behaviors. By assessing the gap, the PBC now has something to move toward, versus dwelling in the past or getting stuck in the current reality (preventing, blaming, or excessive venting).

Assessing the gap can be accomplished with questions like:

- "Tell me what it looks like currently." (Wait for answer)

- "Now, describe your ideal." or "What is the best you can hope for?"

- "On a scale of 1 to 10, with 10 being really good or your ideal, how would you rate where things are at right now?"

- "Using the same scale, where would you like to be?" Optional: "By when?"

- "What are you looking for?"

- "What are you really trying to accomplish here?"
- "If your challenge were removed, what would things look like?"

InDiCom Coaching Model
Stage II: Discover

Discover is the heart of the coaching conversation. Once the purpose and expectations have been clarified and the initial gap assessed, it is time to explore and discover the real issue at hand (root causes). It is common that the initial topic identified in the Involve stage is not the real issue that needs to be solved. It is not until you get into the Discover stage that you will be able to uncover the real issue or root cause of an issue. The Discover stage is where the PBC explores alternative solutions and brainstorms options. The Discover stage is also where you help the PBC close the gap between the current state and the ideal state. It is where the PBC determines *what* he or she is trying to accomplish and *how* to go about accomplishing it. Although action planning doesn't happen yet (that is Stage 3), the PBC should be clear on the direction he or she will move by the time he or she leaves the Discover stage.

The emphasis in the Discover stage is to develop information that leads to a common understanding of and the probable causes of a problem, help the PBC discover possible solutions, explore strategies for solving each issue or concern, and learn where and how to obtain new knowledge, skills, or information that will help the PBC move forward as part of his or her solution or action plan. Whatever topic or content is being discussed, the primary outcome of Stage II is for the PBC to experience ah-ha moments and shifts in his or her thinking, which will ultimately result in constructive action.

Although there are only two goals that the coach should have in mind at the Discover stage, you will spend the majority of time in your coaching conversations here. Each goal should be met before you move the coaching conversation to the final stage. The two critical goals at the Discover stage require you to help the PBC:

- Discover root causes
- Explore alternatives

Discover Root Causes

Discovering root causes often requires the purpose to be redefined. Many issues are not what they seem. Discovering root causes often requires that you probe deeper into the situation. You can do this by remaining focused on the PBC and staying in tune to what is and is not being said. Refrain from jumping to conclusions. Instead, use a more scientific method. Make a hypothesis that you will test by asking probing and open-ended coaching questions. Look for themes or patterns of behavior at a high level. Do this without getting too caught up in the detail of the story. It may not be about what is said as much as what is really happening at an emotional or behavioral level.

One way to discover the root cause is to continue to ask powerful and thought-provoking coaching questions. The tendency is to ask lots of "why" questions, which sound accusatory and put the PBC on the defensive. Avoid "why" questions when you can. The best kinds of questions to ask start with "what" or "how". To demonstrate an appropriate questioning style, refer to the following example:

Let's say the PBC is a human resources manager and identifies his issue as the following: "The department managers don't see me as a strategic partner." You, as the coach, would want to discover the root cause of this issue by asking a variety of questions:

- "What makes you say that?"
- "What do you need from them?"
- "How can you find out what they need from you?"
- "What is your part in this?"
- "How can you improve the relationship?"

The goal is to try to pinpoint the exact issue and to keep the focus on the PBC's role. This puts accountability on the PBC to own his or her part.

We were working with a coaching client who is consistently concerned about her financial liquidity and security. She is regularly stressed about being able to cover payroll, fund her daughter's next semester at school, and a host of other things. In our coaching conversations she often talks about money, how much things cost, how much she spent, how much she gave to x, y, or z charity, or has funneled into one of her start-up businesses. On the surface, the issue seems simple; she needs to get her finances in order, right? Wrong. Without knowing the root cause, this client could never consistently stick to a budget, let alone figure out how to change behaviors to do so. After several coaching sessions and a lot of sharing from the PBC, a pattern of behavior began to emerge. It turns out that she over-commits to everything—her time, energy, resources, services—everything. Including money. The root cause of her problems is over-commitment, not poor spending habits and bad budgeting. The financial piece was only a symptom of a larger issue.

A few of the pivotal coaching questions that we used to get to the root cause were:

- "When have you not been financially strapped?"
- "If you won the lottery, how would things change?"
- "If the financial challenge were removed, what challenges would you still be facing?"
- "You are always at your limit financially. In what other ways are you at your limit?

How did we know that the root cause was over-commitment? We didn't; the PBC put the pieces together and told us!

Now that you have explored and discovered the root cause of what the PBC is trying to solve, it is helpful to have the PBC redefine the issue. This clarifies what the remainder of the coaching conversation will focus on. Have the PBC restate the problem in a way that gives the person ownership over the problem. The PBC should now be able to see that the issue was not exactly what it seemed at first. Even if the difference is subtle, this will change the way the PBC owns the problem and ultimately the action steps that result.

Here are some ways the coach can get the PBC to redefine the issue:

- "Now that you see that you have a part in this, how would you restate what you are trying to do?"

- "What do you think is really going on here?"

- "What else could be contributing to this?"

- "Now that you have discovered the root cause, go back and redefine what you see as the real issue."

- "What do you see now that you didn't see before?"

Explore Alternatives

Successful coaching results when PBCs explore alternatives and discover their own solutions. This seems to be the hardest shift in thinking for coaches to master. Once you have mastered it, you will experience the true power of coaching. Therefore, a critical success factor for becoming a skillful coach is to *not solve* the problem for the PBC.

Coaches are sources of help. Being sources of help, however, does not mean that you know more about a subject than the person you are trying to help. Being a coach means that you are a master of the coaching *process* and that you have the skills to create and maintain a successful coaching interaction. Coaching is the process of *helping others discover what they already know*, not of being the expert.

A successful coaching conversation should never preempt the PBC's initiative or create dependence on the coach. The strength of coaching lies in the fact that coaches are potential resources, not problem solvers. But this very fact can also be a weakness. The best people in every organization are problem solvers. Therefore, it is natural for the coach to *want* to play that role. Problem solvers have been rewarded and promoted because they have demonstrated their ability to solve problems.

The more qualified a person is in solving problems, the more that person will take the lead in solving the problems of others—even when he or she should not do so. Even though the coach's role is to help the PBC discover creative solutions to his or her own problems, it is important to note that the coach's role is not to be the rewarded problem solver, but to place the PBC in that role so he or she is recognized and rewarded for solving his or her own problems. This is part of being *egoless*.

Because it is human nature for the coach to want to help be the expert or consultant by providing advice or teaching the PBC new skills or learning, you must learn to focus on the fact that the PBC needs to own and experience both *"what* needs to be solved" and *"how* to solve it." Through experience is how people learn! And this new learning is best achieved if the PBC is encouraged to stretch and discover his or her own solutions.

As a coach, recognize the need of others to experience their own successes, make and learn from mistakes, and to implement their own ideas and solutions to problems and situations. You wouldn't be where you are today if someone hadn't allowed and encouraged you to try new things and let you do it your way. Give the PBC the same privilege.

Will Rogers said it best, "There are three kinds of men: the ones that learn by reading, the few who learn by observation, and the rest of them have to pee on the electric fence for themselves."

Some of you will likely struggle with letting go of your solutions. Especially if your business is one where mistakes cannot be made without affecting the bottom line. Thus, you may be even more inclined to tell people what to do, believe your solution is best, or come from the perspective that you have been there, done that, and they should learn from your mistakes—after all, you are just trying to prevent them from feeling the awful effects of a failure—right? Coaches understand that by "saving people" they are also depriving them of valuable learning. Let's revisit the notion of commitment from Chapter 1:

"Commitment, like motivation, is not something that you can observe directly. You infer that it exists because of what people

do. You say that people are 'committed' when they demonstrate over and over again their determination to do their best
and their unwillingness to give up in the face of obstacles.
Committed people in organizations are tied intellectually and
emotionally to the values and goals of the organization. Committed people know what they are doing, and they believe that
what they are doing is important. People cannot become committed to what is vague or trivial."

In this case, in order for people to be committed to an action or to
changing a behavior, they must buy in. Commitment is not achieved
through people doing as they are told. People are committed to *their*
ideas.

Coaches often head straight for disaster when they do not allow
the PBC to generate solutions for him- or herself. In addition, because
"We teach others how to treat us" (McGraw, 1999), you have likely
taught your team members that you *do* have all the answers and if
they just wait you out or dodge your questions long enough, you will
give them the answers. Your new challenge will be learning how to ask
the right questions and outwait them! Therefore, learn how to make
this transition. Start using some of the following questions to keep the
focus on the PBC solving the issue, not on you solving it.

- "If you were to give advice to someone in your situation,
  what would it be?"
- "What would you tell somebody in your shoes if he or she
  asked you how to fix this problem?"
- "Have you ever experienced something similar to this that you
  could draw from?"
- "What would you do if you did know the answer?"
- "What would your best friend tell you to do?"

If someone is really stuck, encourage him or her to think of someone (a previous boss, leader, or friend) who modeled what he or she is

trying to achieve. Once the PBC exhausts his or her own ideas and solutions first, then and *only* then can you offer a solution of your own. Although giving advice should be avoided, there may be a few circumstances in which it is helpful or necessary. In order to help the PBC get unstuck, qualify it with something like, "Would you like my advice?" or "Could you imagine yourself saying (doing) . . .?" We encourage you to ask permission to see whether the PBC wants your advice first. For example, "These are great solutions that you came up with. I had another one come to mind if you'd like to hear it." Most of the time the PBC will say, "Yes." What you are actually doing is showing respect to the coaching relationship by offering your ideas, not forcing them, and offering another alternative, not providing the ultimate solution. But remember, *only* do this after you've given the PBC the opportunity and time to do it on his or her own. This takes discipline. You should not assume that the solution you suggest will be the one the PBC will choose to implement. The purpose of your input is to get the PBC unstuck in their thinking. Thus, it can be even more helpful if you follow your proposed idea with another question such as, "Now, what might work for you in this situation?"

As you try to get the PBC unstuck in determining solutions, here are some questions that might help:

- "What ideas or solutions have you thought of already?"
- "What options do you have?"
- "Share with me at least three possible solutions."
- "What shift in thinking did you need to make?"
- "What information will you need to gather to move forward?"
- "Who/what are your resources?"
- "What would you try if there were no rules?"

The coaching model is focused on the PBC's ideas and solutions, not on yours. This does not mean that you let people flounder or set them up to fail. If someone needs specific information, direction, or guidance, don't coach; instead provide it using another role. When you play the *coach role*, coach! Remember, the *coach role* requires you to make a mental shift so that the PBC determines both *what* (he or she is going to do) and *how* (he or she will do it).

InDiCom Coaching Model
Stage III: Commit

The overarching goal of coaching is to achieve commitment to sustained superior performance—while maintaining positive work relationships. The entire coaching process leads toward this goal, and it all comes together in Stage III as the PBC reaches a new level of commitment. Thus, the third and final stage of the InDiCom coaching model is all about moving the PBC to commitment.

The purpose of this stage is for the PBC to walk away with a clear plan of action. A plan that the PBC believes in, is energized by, and committed to. Once an action plan has been identified, the PBC's commitment to the plan can be strengthened by identifying and eliminating roadblocks and obstacles that might interfere with the PBC's ability to successfully carry it out. Final comments are also in order as you close the coaching conversation. Each coaching conversation should have a sense of completeness and closure, and it is your role to make sure this happens. Part of this closure is to solicit feedback from the PBC as to when follow-up or progress checks will occur.

The goals at this stage are to have the PBC:

- Create an action plan
- Eliminate roadblocks and obstacles
- Recap

Create an Action Plan

Creating an action plan means the PBC identifies what steps or course of action is required to solve the issues discussed and move forward.

Creating an action plan can take a number of different forms. The PBC may focus solely on the first or next step that needs to be taken. Or, the action plan may include a list of action items, random or sequential, that the PBC identifies. It may consist of a "dry run" where the coach and PBC have an opportunity to role play or act out parts of an impending conversation.

Action planning can be as simple as having the PBC try out some new learning and then check back with you. Or it can be as complicated as a five- or ten-year career development sequence. More complicated plans may include high-level goals with sub-goals, each requiring several steps and short- and long-term action items. It can include tasks such as putting together a revised project schedule or writing a proposal.

Whatever the content or complexity of an action plan, good plans tend to have the following characteristics:

- The PBC assumes all responsibility for the plan and the plan is a reflection of his or her input and decisions. (*Note:* if the PBC doesn't write down the plan or take notes, that is his or her prerogative.)

- Action plans include concrete, observable behaviors and do more than convey vague intentions such as "try harder," "learn that skill," "get my numbers up," "be more sensitive," or "pay more attention."

- Action plans ultimately (not necessarily in one conversation) have short- and long-term goals.

- Action plans have a built-in means of measuring progress and success in the future.

Included in the next steps should be some provision for keeping the coach informed of the PBC's progress. Some coaches do a very credible job of confronting the issue only to lose the payoff because they do not pay sufficient attention to planning or because they take back ownership that doesn't belong to them by trying to plan the PBC's actions after a viable solution is discovered. Planning does not mean that PBCs merely indicate that they will correct a problem or improve proficiency. Voiced intentions to correct a problem or obtain a skill have limited value. Make sure that the PBC identifies a set of specific actions to solve the problem or improve proficiency. This is part of the *what* and *how*.

PBC (vague response): "I will get right on the budget submission, and I'll let you know immediately if I still run into problems that will keep me from meeting the new deadline."

PBC (specific response): "The first thing I am going to do is review the contract provisions with the supplier. I'll let the team know if that doesn't solve our problem of noncompliance and I will report back to you on Friday."

What actions can you take as coach to solicit more specific responses? Here are some questions you can use.

- "What is the first thing you can do to put your plan into action?"
- "Specifically, what do you need to do to accomplish that?"
- "How can you start?"
- "Tell me your plan."

Ask the PBC to share his or her action plan or next steps with you. The following are examples of statements you can expect to hear to ensure successful planning. At the end of each action plan statement, there is a sample reply from the coach that illustrates supportiveness and shows how the onus of follow-up remains with the PBC.

PBC: "I'm going to try my new approach with Deid rick, giving him more latitude in the sequence that he uses in handling applications. I'm going to see how it goes for a week."

COACH: "This sounds like something new for you and I'm glad you're willing to give it a shot. I'm really interested in hearing how it goes; when would you like to get back together with me so you can share how it went?"

PBC: "I'm going to find out from our rate clerks exactly what they do, what they like, and what they don't like; then, I can see whether I want to make that move."

COACH: "That's a great idea and should provide the insight you are looking for to make your decision. When can you provide me with a status report?"

PBC: "I'm definitely seeing the design shop with a new perspective and I know I should get more involved so I don't continue to have the conflict that seems to develop when the fabrication shop receives a design. The first thing I'm going to do is talk with the design shop manager and find out how our team can make the transition smoother."

COACH: "Talking with the design shop manager is a great first step. I am interested in hearing what you learn. When will you be able to share something with me?"

Eliminate Roadblocks and Obstacles

By having the PBC identify roadblocks or potential obstacles and how to overcome them, you increase the level of commitment to the chosen course of action and the person's confidence to follow through with the plan. By asking questions that identify roadblocks and obstacles, you allow the PBC to explore options to get around, over, or through them. Now, the PBC can go forth with confidence knowing that if he or she encounters a roadblock or obstacle, there is a plan to overcome it. Even if an obstacle comes up that has *not* been identified and examined, the PBC will be better equipped to overcome it.

Sometimes, the PBC might say that there are no obstacles. While this may be the case, you should ensure that the PBC is looking from all angles and, if appropriate, play a qualified game of devil's advocate, but in the end, it is the PBC's call. If the PBC truly doesn't see any obstacles, accept this as fact and move on.

You may also ask the PBC to assess any risks associated with the current plan or solution and determine whether any fine-tuning is needed. By adding the exploration of roadblocks, obstacles, and risks to the coaching conversation, you are equipping the PBC to be successful in the implementation of his or her action plan. Removing obstacles can be essential to the PBC's success. To eliminate roadblocks and obstacles, ask questions like these:

- "Is there anything else you need to consider?"
- "You sound very committed to your plan. What might interfere with being able to carry it out?"
- "What can you do to ensure your plan of action will be successful?"
- "How can you keep the consequences to a minimum?"
- "What could you put in place as a back-up plan?"
- "What roadblocks do you foresee that you should think about now?"
- "What obstacles will you face?" . . . "How will you overcome these?"
- "Are there things you haven't thought of?"

Recap

Recap describes the process of completing the coaching conversation. The goal is to reinforce the PBC's sense of achievement and obtain commitment. The recap is provided by the PBC, and the coach affirms the PBC's response and ensures a follow-up plan is in place.

Even if you only have a minute remaining, do not skip the recap! The recap only takes a moment and it encapsulates the entire coaching conversation into a few sentences. It solidifies the coaching process and secures a commitment to action on the part of the PBC, which was the ultimate goal that you were trying to achieve.

Having the PBC provide a recap of the coaching conversation is the most successful and powerful way to close a coaching conversation.

The PBC should provide a sentence or two that summarizes what has been accomplished, learnings that have occurred, next steps, and what agreements and commitments have been made. The recap ensures common understanding and reinforces what the PBC has achieved. Recap builds a sense of completeness and closure. Recapping is particularly important when the coaching conversation was centered on a performance problem. A recap statement ensures clarity at the end of a conversation, during which different points of view may have emerged. The recap helps achieve the goal of closure and encourages a demonstration of the PBC's commitment.

An added benefit to the recap is that you will typically hear excitement and energy in the person's voice. You will feel the PBC's renewed sense of energy, and this is where you know that you have played the *coach role* successfully. This is one of your rewards as a coach!

How does the recap work? The coach starts it out by saying something like:

- "Summarize in a sentence or two what you are taking away from today."

- "I know we only have a minute or two; in that time share with me your key learnings from today."

- "Take a moment to highlight what you learned today."

- "Recap for me what we've agreed on."

Replies from the PBC may sound like:

- "I think I've done a good job identifying the main reasons that I'm behind in getting the new proposal out. Although it's already late, I know what I need to do with the team to get the proposal out by next week. I didn't realize that I was the only one holding it up, but now I know what to do. I will start by reviewing the proposal requirements."

- "I have a strategy together for our meeting with the Personnel Advisory Committee. First, I won't take the lead in attacking the new time card policy. This is the general manager's own idea, so I need to go softly. Second, if the policy is brought up, I will comment first on its positive features. Third, when they do start talking about changes, I will make sure that I show how the changes I want are primarily ways of cutting down paperwork."

- "Now I know how our team should behave in these technical reviews with the suppliers: First, we should give a brief statement of what we have found that needs to be changed and the data to support the need. I will ensure that happens. Second, we should always make a recommendation of how to fix what we think is wrong. I will make sure the team prepares for this in advance of the meetings."

- "When you first brought up the topic, I wasn't sure if I agreed with you that anything needed to be addressed. I had my point of view and you had yours about what is happening as we change to the new team concept for customer service. I think, however, that I've identified the basic issue: my team can't spend the time we need to develop our service team and still have time to give our customers what they want. What I need to do now is figure out a plan that will get our team up and running without damaging our customer relations, and I want the team's input on how to do that."

- "The first thing I need to do is start being their leader. I need to let go of some of this control. I'm going to start out by having the team determine our meeting agendas and letting them run more of the meeting. Then, I'm going to. . . ."

Your response to the PBC's recap should include use of the *encourage* skill (Chapter 6) to validate and affirm, as well as support the PBC's learnings, action plan, progress, and/or commitment to action. Feeling appreciated is one of the four critical elements that builds commitment (see Chapter 1). Your role is to always end with a celebrate (*encourage* skill) statement so the PBC feels appreciated.

A performance coaching conversation (Chapter 7) can easily leave the PBC with some unresolved negative feelings. It is important that coaches end a performance coaching session with positive comments about the PBC's strengths or efforts that he or she has made during the coaching interaction. The goal, of course, is to leave the PBC with a positive belief in him- or herself and capacity to succeed. (Read more about Performance Coaching in Chapter 7.)

Closing comments from the coach that express appreciation sound like:

- "I know it wasn't easy for you to dig into the causes for the team's poor performance this quarter. You have done a fine job of analysis, and based on your explanation I now see your team has shown a lot of courage in what they've done."

- "You're really developing a feel for what makes your division work. The group you partner with is a different breed and you're clearly getting a handle on what makes them tick."

- "You've already shown that you have the skills to take the lead in our next research project, and I know that you have more knowledge of how to design surveys than nearly anyone else around. I'm delighted to know that you're interested in the role."

- "I know that this conversation has been tough for you. You have been very candid and forthright in describing how you got into this difficulty. I have all the confidence in the world that you can fix the problem and prevent it from happening again."

- "It has always been clear to me that you care a great deal about keeping the people in purchasing happy. Your proposal to have weekly status meetings with them is a great step in the right direction."

Each conversation should end with final closing words, which can be provided by either the PBC or coach. These should include a confirmation of any follow-up meetings, like the following examples:

Coach

- "When would you like to touch base again and review your progress?"

- "Your insights today were brilliant, and I think you have a great course of action laid out. I look forward to hearing how it went when we meet again next month, third Friday, back here in your office."

- "I am very impressed with what you discovered about yourself today; that took a lot of guts on your part. I'm proud of you and can't wait to hear how it goes when we meet again next week."

- "I really enjoy working with you! You're eager to learn and pick things up so quickly. When can you call me to let me know how it goes?"

PBC

- "Can we meet again next week so I can tell you about my progress?"

- "I'll be excited to get back together with you in a month to share what happens."

- "I know you're busy, but if it's okay with you, can we meet in a few days so that I can figure out more of this mess?"

Each successful coaching conversation creates a sense of closure or completeness. If closure is not achieved at the end of a coaching conversation, the PBC may feel that nothing has been accomplished, that the conversation has been irrelevant, or that he or she was not given an opportunity to communicate concerns. Closure can occur even if more sessions are scheduled to address the same issue.

In every coaching conversation, closure occurs when people feel that they have experienced an ah-ha moment or they have learned something new. In a session that confronts unsatisfactory performance, the PBC has a sense of closure if the problem has been accurately identified and progress has been made to resolve it. The coach should be satisfied if the PBC moved from A to B. B to Z can come later.

Even if you are short on time, *do not skip* the recap or the closing words. Shorten if you have to, but don't skip them. The recap not only solidifies the entire coaching process. It also helps to achieve what you were ultimately striving for: "Coaching for Commitment."

Coaching is a process, not an event. Not all coaching conversations accomplish all that is needed in one session. Coaching is often a series of sessions, each dealing with a specific narrower topic in order to reach a broader goal. Multiple sessions are sometimes needed for persons coached to finish acquiring a set of skills, to find out more information, or to finish exploring the causes for some problem. Each conversation should still provide closure to the topic of that session.

Interdependent Stages

As mentioned previously, although the stages of the InDiCom coaching model appear linear in nature, they are not. The stages mark the transition from one set of goals to the next. As you use the process, you will sometimes find yourself moving from one stage to the next, only to realize that the real issue surfaces later in the conversation, thus requiring you, as the coach, to move back to a previous stage. Often, the real issue or underlying cause surfaces just as you think a coaching session is ending, thus requiring you to recycle back through the whole process. This is normal.

The InDiCom coaching model is actually a cyclical and iterative process (see Figure 5.3). This means that you may jump back and forth between stages. As you just learned, when you enter into a coaching conversation, the purpose and expectations are clarified up-front. All too commonly, it's not until you spend time in the *Discover* stage that you figure out what the real issue is and realize that you must explore it, instead of the original one you were pursuing. At this

Figure 5.3. Iterative Process of Coaching

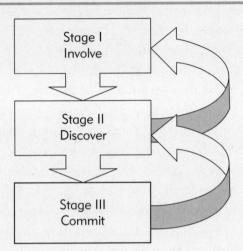

point, the new issue now requires that the purpose and expectations to be reclarified.

Once Stage I is completed for a second time, move to Discover for a second iteration. These iterations will be repeated so long as the problem definition is modified and until the coach and the PBC have accurately identified and agreed on the real issue. Clearly defining the issue becomes the first priority for being resolved. The coaching process can jump back and forth between stages at any time, but ultimately you will want to progress to the Commit stage.

Coaching Moment

Current State: How are you currently conducting your coaching conversations? Identify the parts of the InDiCom model that you are using in your current approach (reflect on the InDiCom goals as well as the stages).

Ideal State: What steps of the model are missing from your current approach? Think about the coaching conversations you have within any given day. (Also include the conversations that you may not normally think of as coaching.) Specifically, which ones could benefit by applying a process such as the InDiCom coaching model?

Action Plan: What can you do in order to more closely follow the InDiCom model in your next conversation?

Chapter Summary

The InDiCom coaching model is the piece of the Coaching Prism that guides a coach through the stages of a coaching conversation. InDiCom (pronounced In-dee-com) stands for the three stages of the model.

Involve is all about getting the PBC involved in the coaching conversation by clarifying the purpose and expectations of the conversation, establishing ownership and agreement, and assessing the gap.

Discover is about discovering root causes (core issues), exploring alternatives and creative solutions, and gathering insight on the gap that the PBC is trying to close.

Commit is about the action planning on the part of the PBC, removing obstacles and barriers, and successfully closing the coaching conversation with a recap that is provided by the PBC.

All stages of the process are interdependent, and though there is typically movement back and forth between the stages, conversations are intended to move the PBC forward toward specific results and closure.

It is the application of the InDiCom coaching model that leads to a commitment to higher performance while maintaining positive work relationships.

CHAPTER 6

CLEAR Coaching Skills

"If I had more skill in what I'm attempting, I wouldn't need so much courage."

—Ashleigh Brilliant

THE CLEAR COACHING SKILLS illustrated in the Coaching Prism (see Figure 6.1), are common, everyday communication techniques you already use when interacting with others. By creating a conscious awareness around your use of these skills, you will learn how to increase the effectiveness of your coaching conversations.

Being clear and concise is critical to many aspects of the coaching conversation. For that reason, coaching and clarity go hand-in-hand. Thus, the acronym CLEAR was created to represent the coaching skills because it acts as a constant reminder to you as the coach to be CLEAR.

You may notice some crossover between these skills and material already covered in the book. This is because so many of the elements of coaching and its competencies are interrelated. Each of the CLEAR

Figure 6.1. Coaching Prism

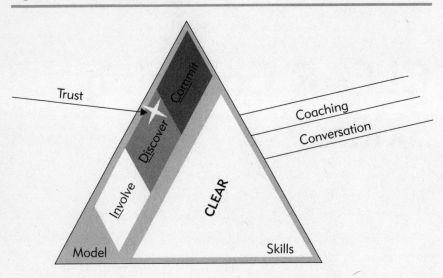

skills has its own merit, and we encourage you to study them as if they were new to you.

Some skills are easier to learn and use than others. Determining which are easy and which are harder is in the eye of the beholder. Some will come naturally to you, and others will require more practice. Incorporate the easy skills into your coaching conversations first, then slowly add the more challenging skills to your repertoire.

Using CLEAR coaching skills within the coaching conversation allows you to facilitate the creation of ah-ha moments for the person being coached (PBC). Further, it allows PBCs to see different perspectives as well as to think differently and creatively so that they can ultimately come up with their own solutions and ideas that will achieve commitment to sustained superior performance.

The CLEAR coaching skills are used throughout all stages of the InDiCom coaching model and should be applied throughout your coaching conversations. Some skills will be used more frequently than others. These skills can be applied to any channel of coaching, whether it is face-to-face or virtual (by phone, teleconference, video conference, or email). Channels of coaching are discussed in greater detail in Chapter 7.

There are five CLEAR coaching skills for you to master. Each skill corresponds to a letter in the CLEAR acronym:

- Challenge
- Listen
- Encourage
- Ask
- Refine

For some, these skills will simply be an effective reminder. For others, using these skills as they are prescribed here may require a shift in the way you currently think and behave when in the *coach role*. Because coaching is holistic in its approach and results-oriented in its outcomes, *using* CLEAR will help you to *be* clear, have more successful coaching conversations, and have more committed PBCs.

Challenge

Challenge
Listen
Encourage
Ask
Refine

Let's get started with Challenge. All of the techniques used to present the PBC with a meaningful Challenge are challenging themselves—challenging because they ask the coach to be diligent, present in the moment, and willing to challenge the PBC's status quo.

Challenge is about helping the PBC experience an ah-ha moment or a shift in his or her own thinking. It is used when the PBC is stuck and needs a little push or when the PBC requires feedback regarding incongruence or a disconnect between behaviors or comments. The purpose of Challenge is to provide PBCs with insight that will help them move forward or away from an impending disaster.

How do you go about using the skill of Challenge? Most commonly, you will use your *intuition* to determine when the Challenge skill is needed; then you will deliver the message by way of making a request or by providing a reality check.

Intuition

Have you ever been walking or driving alone in an unfamiliar place when suddenly something tells you that you are in the wrong place at the wrong time? What do you do? Stay there and wait to see if you're right? Or do you change direction, pick up your pace, and head for a place that feels safer? Most people would take the latter route, choosing to get out of there, not worrying about whether they were right or wrong.

What about at work? Have you ever had a conversation with someone that on the surface seemed quite ordinary, but you had a nagging feeling that something was awry? This is an example of your *intuition* at work Did you tell the person what you were thinking, or did you continue on with the conversation as if nothing had changed?

How often do you pay attention to your intuition? It may be that little voice inside your head, your racing heart, or a feeling in the pit of your stomach that acts as a sixth sense. What happens to you at those moments when your intuition kicks in? Do you acknowledge and give life to it, or do you second-guess yourself and dismiss it? ("No, that can't be right, I must be imagining things.")

Think of intuition like an alarm clock. The clock goes off and you have two choices: wake up or hit the snooze button; address it or ignore it. By choosing to address it, you are making the choice to take action. In coaching, when your intuition goes off, choose to make the coaching conversation more productive by addressing what your intuition is telling you. Intuition helps you discover root causes to issues that would normally go undiscovered or be dealt with at a surface level. Next time your intuition goes off, *wake up*!

One caution about the use of intuition: You have to be willing to be wrong. If your intuition is off-base or the PBC isn't ready to address or make the connection that you have brought to light, let it go and move on. Whatever you do, don't try to convince the PBC that you are right. This is dangerous territory—just as when you were in that unfamiliar place—did it matter whether you were right or wrong in the end? No, it only mattered that you were safe.

Challenge allows the coach to make connections that would not normally be obvious to the PBC. Challenge means connecting the dots by recognizing and telling the PBC when incongruent pieces of the conversation occur and how they fit together to create a different look at reality. In order to be able to pick up on the little things during a coaching conversation and make these connections, you need to be in tune with and able to trust your intuition as well as to act on it and be willing to be wrong if it is off target.

There are times when parts of the coaching conversation (or multiple conversations) may indicate a repeated pattern of behavior that has gone unrecognized. Coaching is *not* therapy, nor does it have to be for you as the coach to call out repetitive patterns of behavior in order to examine how they affect the PBC at work or impede him or her from achieving the ideal goals. In the corporate world, the most destructive of these patterns are referred to as "career derailers" or "stallers," and it is your job as coach to identify them if the PBC does not. Then the PBC can decide whether the pattern applies and how to move forward.

Example of Intuition

Skyler is a senior manager in a highly technical field. She continues to do well and move up in the organization, but has a difficult time addressing conflict without being seen as aggressive. One of her coaching goals is to address conflict more effectively and stop using the overly aggressive approach.

During coaching sessions, the coach recognizes that Skyler occasionally refers to the state of powerlessness she feels in her personal life by making statements like, "My parents moved a lot when I was a kid and now I am at the mercy of my husband's job for my geographical location. I don't know what I will do if we have to move again."

On the surface, not only do Skyler's comments about moving not have much to do with work, but it also does not sound like they have anything to do with her being overly aggressive in dealing with conflict—or do they? The coach's intuition says there is a connection to be made here.

Is it possible that because Skyler doesn't have a say in whether her family moves or not, that she is transferring her home-life frustration to work? Could she be overcompensating for her lack of control at home to how she deals with conflict at work? If so, it may indicate a pattern of behavior that needs to be addressed.

Intuition allows the coach to address these seemingly unrelated items or "dis-connect" by way of the Challenge skill—making a statement or asking a question that will allow Skyler to connect the dots and see a pattern of behavior if one exists. At this point, the coach might say:

COACH/BRUCE: "Skyler, it seems like your inability to control what happens in your personal life is affecting your interactions at work."

PBC/SKYLER: "Oh my gosh, Bruce, you're right! I guess because I don't get a say at home about moving and a lot of other things, I bottle up all of my frustration up. Then, when I come to work and a conflict occurs, I just blow my top! I find myself being really angry but . . . it isn't really about the work stuff. It's more because I feel like my opinion doesn't count at home. Here, I guess I feel more in control so I get carried away and try to make sure I don't lose the ability to have a say by being forceful. Maybe too forceful."

Ah-ha! Now that a pattern of behavior has been recognized, this is the start of a new turn in the coaching conversation, which allows the coach to ask questions that will move Skyler forward toward her goal. (Because coaching is not therapy, the focus now remains on the future and on work interactions, not on the past and the family dynamic.) You may start with something like:

COACH/BRUCE: "I'm glad that you were able to recognize this pattern. How can this realization help you with your goal of handling conflict more effectively at work?"

The beauty of coaching is that there may also be positive by-products that occur at home from such a revelation!

Had the coach not followed her intuition, Skyler might still be stuck in the problem rather than moving forward and committing to actions that solve it. Using intuition is not a "woo-woo" practice. It is an advanced technique used by coaches to unearth root causes.

Note that if Skyler disagreed with the coach or chose not to address the situation in this way, the coach would accept her response without argument and move on.

Here are some other sample statements to illustrate addressing *intuition*:

- "From everything you've said, it appears that you are really tough on yourself." (Wait for confirmation.)

- "We were talking about the problems you are having with the new spreadsheet, but it seems what's most on your mind is your disappointment about not receiving the bonus you expected. Do you want to take a minute to discuss this first?"

- "What are you getting out of this?"

- "What are you avoiding/ignoring?"

Be in touch with your intuition. Use it to uncover a disconnect, and then use requests and reality checks as successful techniques for delivering a well-needed message that Challenges the PBC. The combination of using your *intuition, reality checks,* and *requests* is powerful for discovering root causes. Let your intuition be your guide.

Request

Request is a Challenge that moves the PBC out of his or her comfort zone or challenges the status quo. A *request* is a statement or question that encourages the PBC to take a risk or stretch out of the comfort zone in order to learn a new skill, understand what it's like to be in someone else's shoes, and eliminate or face fears.

Request is an advanced technique because it should not be used lightly or carelessly by the coach. The coach should be well aware of the possibilities (good and bad) when making a request of someone. Be prepared to support the PBC, regardless of the outcome.

Never make a request as a means of getting your own hidden agenda met. In other words, the request should be made solely for the benefit of the PBC. Delegating or assigning a task is not a request; it is a managerial directive (to be used when in the *manager role*). Requests, on the other hand, provide PBCs with a risk or Challenge in order to promote their growth and skill. The motivations for each are distinctly different. In addition, with a request, the PBC is given freedom of negotiation and action.

Creating an environment that encourages risk taking (within reason) allows people to learn from mistakes, versus suffer because of them. Such an environment makes acting on requests comfortable and safe. When a fear ("I am afraid to . . .") is undermining a solution, the coach can effectively use a request to address the fear.

Sample Requests

- If the PBC cannot manage to get through a team meeting without correcting a colleague or direct report, it may be appropriate to Challenge the person, to not speak at all, or speak only when spoken to during the next meeting.

- If the PBC constantly tells (fixes) versus asks when in the *coach role* with others, it could be useful for the person to try only asking questions for an entire day (more challenging: ask the person to do this at home as well as work).

- If the PBC has a personality conflict with a peer, it may be appropriate to request that he or she take that person out to lunch or for coffee, with a goal of finding a common interest.

- If the PBC is someone who feels he or she doesn't receive enough recognition from a manager, encourage him or her to model what he or she wants by finding a reason to compliment the boss, first!

- If the PBC aspires to become a project manager but has never tried complex project management, try requesting that he or she take on a small, simple project to test his or her skills and ability (PBC chooses project).

- If a PBC has a fear of failure or is a perfectionist, it may be appropriate to Challenge or request that he or she fail at something, anything, during the next week. This doesn't have to be big or reckless.

- If the PBC is struggling with diversity issues, it might be worthwhile to make a request that he or she do some volunteering at an organization that embodies what he or she does not understand.

- If the PBC is struggling with rejection or not being included, make it a request that the PBC try to receive ten rejections within one week or day. He or she may find it is harder to be rejected than once thought!

All of these are effective ways to create ah-ha moments for the PBC, which allows him or her to see the results of trying something in a new way. A request does not direct the outcome; rather, it encourages exploration of the unknown. Of course, this technique doesn't stop with the request; the next coaching conversation should contain dialogue around what the benefits were to the PBC for trying the new behavior. It should also contain encouragement and celebration for the accomplishment and effort put forth to take on the Challenge.

Use the request graphic in Figure 6.2 as a guide when making a request of a PBC. Prepare the PBC by letting him or her know that you are making a request and explain the options (especially if this is the first time you have made a request of this PBC). The PBC may either accept your Challenge or renegotiate the terms. If the PBC chooses to renegotiate, he or she may make a counter-offer stating what he or she will do instead. You both will agree to the terms and follow up, with the PBC reporting back progress or learnings to the coach. Be in tune to the PBC's response when making the request.

Figure 6.2. Request

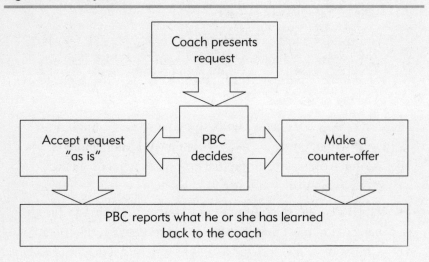

Reality Check

There are times when coaches can and should serve as a resource for removing blind spots and someone who provides hard-hitting, non-judgmental feedback to the PBC. This is called a *reality check*. If the coach sees or hears a critical disconnect in what the PBC is saying versus doing, sees a blind spot that the PBC refuses to see or acknowledge, if the coach identifies a recurring pattern of behavior or sometimes when the coach's intuition simply kicks in and says, "Pay attention, something is going on here," the coach should make one attempt to call the PBC on the behavior.

A reality check is a short, succinct, statement, not always a question, that addresses the issue. If the coach is wrong, the PBC may immediately say, "No, that's not it." The coach should not come back and try to force his or her own perspective on the PBC, but should return to where the conversation left off. If the coach nails the issue on the head, the PBC will usually remain silent for a moment before saying anything (allow this silence to happen), or may quickly affirm your comment. When a PBC experiences an ah-ha moment that will have a lasting impact on his or her way of thinking and behaviors, it is truly magical to experience.

In the example given earlier in the chapter, where Skyler wanted to stop being so aggressive at work, her coach made a reality check statement that allowed Skyler to see how what was going on at home was affecting her behavior at work:

COACH/BRUCE: "Skyler, it seems like your inability to control what happens in your personal life is affecting your interactions at work."

Following are additional samples of reality check statements. More sample reality checks can be found in Appendix B.

Sample Reality Checks

- "You keep telling me that you trust your employees. Do you realize that everything you are doing is micro-management, indicating that you really don't trust them?"
- "You are so competitive that you're even competing with your wife on vacation!"
- "Your employees are so dependent on your approval, you're paralyzing them."
- "It's not surprising that you don't reward or recognize your employees, since you don't require recognition yourself."
- "You are taking on so much responsibility for your team's success that you are actually doing more harm than good."
- "You are trying to save everyone from feeling the pain of the upcoming changes."
- "It appears you are playing the role of mother to your employees more than the role of leader."
- "You are operating out of fear."
- "It appears you are more concerned with seeking your boss's approval than managing your team."

As mentioned in Chapter 4, one tip for making a reality check statement easier is following the motto: "Say what you mean, but don't say it mean." (And how the other person takes it is up to him or her.) As well-known author Spencer Johnson, M.D., said, "Integrity is telling ourselves the truth, and honesty is telling the truth to other people." To deliver a reality check, use a child's brand of honesty, one that is not intended to cause harm or to insult others, only to express what was observed. Skillful coaches express what they observe without judgment.

Reality checks prevent PBCs from being sheltered from the truth and keep them from being enabled or dependent on others to survive and succeed.

Being a coach is not always about being nice; it is about understanding and caring about the success of those you are coaching. Sometimes, caring means sharing the obvious and sometimes the uncomfortable. Avoidance is not kindness, it is cowardly. If situations need to be addressed, confronting them in a timely and direct manner using a reality check can have far greater results than pretending they will go away. We all know ignoring bad behavior does not make it go away. In fact, it usually makes it worse.

Listen

Challenge
Listen
Encourage
Ask
Refine

Did you ever wonder why listening has become a component of many leadership courses and why there are so many types of listening? Listening for understanding, focused listening, active listening, appreciative listening, evaluative listening, and the list goes on. It's because listening is harder than it sounds, it requires energy, and most people are average listeners, at best!

Think of Listen as a workout for the brain! The average person speaks at a rate of 125 to 175 words per minute, yet we can listen at a rate of 450 words per minute (Carver, Johnson, & Friedman, 1970), and we think at 1,000 to 3,000 words per minute (HighGain, 2000). So what fills the space between what is being said by the PBC and heard by the coach? Are you thinking of your next question? Formulating solutions? Creating a to-do list? Preparing an agenda for your next meeting? Putting together your shopping list? Or . . . Geez! What *is* that annoying noise down the hall?

Speaking of noise, listening not only includes what is being verbalized to you but also the things you hear without realizing it. The radio in the next cubical, the clock ticking, the phone ringing in the distance, your PDA vibrating, or your email indicator notice. And what about those daydreams? There is always a precise moment when you suddenly realize you've lost all connections to the current conversation and that you haven't been listening for who knows how long?

Take a moment right now and evaluate your own listening skills by responding to the following questions with a **yes** or **no** answer:

_____ I eliminate as many distractions as I can during one-on-one meetings.

_____ I listen with a purpose, looking for key points, emotions, or meaning.

_____ I often repeat what is being said in my head.

_____ I am aware of when I stop listening.

_____ I am able to correctly reflect or summarize what a speaker has said.

_____ When I find myself drifting, I immediately refocus my attention back on the speaker.

_____ When a speaker hits an emotional chord with me, I am able to refocus and adjust so that I hear the remainder of what is said.

_____ I am willing to let someone know if I have stopped listening and ask the person to repeat information.

_____ I listen for clues that tell me if what is being said
matches the body language, tone, intention, and pauses
of the speaker.

If you can answer yes to all of these questions, congratulations!
You are likely to be a very effective listener and the people you are
coaching are lucky to have you as their coach. Lots of "yes" responses
mean you are listening and not bored with the conversations or just
waiting to talk, or worse yet, to interrupt! Most people fight an uphill
battle because listening and remaining focused is work. The average
adult attention span is anywhere from six to twenty minutes (depending on the source). How long do you think yours is? Are there dimin-
ishing factors that would lessen it further? What do you do to eliminate
distractions? How do you stay focused during conversations?

If you struggled with answering these statements affirmatively,
you are not alone! You can still be an effective coach if you are willing
to take a good honest look at your listening skills and commit to
improving them. Mastering the following techniques will help, and if
you know people with impeccable listening skills, observe them in
action, ask them their secrets. Then start to build your own plan of
action for more effective listening.

How to Listen

When in the *coach role*, Listen to more than just the words being said.
This requires you to be diligent in talking less and paying close attention to non-verbal clues both in face-to-face interactions and virtually.
During a coaching conversation, listen for what *is not* said, as much as
what *is* said. Coaches who Listen display the following behaviors:

- They are present and focused on the PBC.

- They show respect in their own verbal and non-verbal dialog.

- They let the PBC know they are being heard and understood.

- They don't multitask (turn off monitors/computers/cell phones,
  forward the phone, and do not do email while virtual coaching).

- They don't make assumptions.

Coaches hear main ideas, key points, changes in tone, and unnatural pauses and are able to ascertain strengths, values, wants, and needs of the PBC. Coaches Listen without evaluating by making sure that they understand before they try to speak and by not forcing a problem into their own frames of reference (*coaching biases*). The coach does not decide whether what the PBC says is right or wrong, workable or not; it just is.

Coaches Listen during all stages of a conversation in order to understand. One caution about listening is that you must be disciplined in not creating blocks to the free and easy development of a mutual interaction. It is easy to stop listening when you hear something you disagree with and even easier to stop listening as soon as you think you know how to fix a problem for the PBC.

Benefits of Silence

In order to listen, learn how to embrace *silence*.

"Silence is golden." Most of us have heard the phrase; now it's time to put it to use. Silence can be a very useful tool, especially in the world of coaching. Learning to use silence effectively benefits both coach and PBC because it creates space in the conversation for processing and reflection.

The toughest part of this technique is learning that it is okay to have a gap in the conversation that results in silence. These gaps, often viewed as "awkward moments," do not have to be uncomfortable. If you are a coach who typically fills the space with talk, today is the day to commit to silence. It is appropriate to allow silence in a conversation when:

- The PBC requires time to think, strategize, or process: "This is a lot to process at once; take your time." (Pause.)

- The coach is looking for agreement on the PBC's accountability to a shared goal: "Last week, we agreed you would be on time for work every day this week. You have already been late twice." (Pause and wait for a response no matter how long it takes.)

- The coach is trying to listen and needs time to reflect on what was just said so he can ask the best question: "I'd like a moment to think about what you just said." (Pause.)

If you struggle with silence, count (in your head) 1, 2, 3, 4 . . . for however long it takes for the PBC to process. Remember, listening is physical work and it requires that you listen to more than just the words spoken. It also means that you learn when and how to effectively use silence. (This is especially important when coaching by phone.)

Story Telling

Encourage and solicit stories from the PBC. People who get to tell stories are more apt to reveal information that they may not normally share, and in many cases, a good coach (who is mentally present during the coaching conversation) can ascertain useful information from what is being said. *Story telling* can help the coach to better understand context, gaps, the PBC's values, strengths, and needs as well as what is going on under the surface of a situation. Story telling is a great way of engaging a listener, in this case, you. People learn better through stories.

The following are just a few examples of how a story can tell a coach more about the PBC:

- A person who is animated and uses humor when telling a story might have a light-hearted nature and need to have fun at work.

- A person who uses mostly words with a negative connotation or who always plays devil's advocate may be a perfectionist who has a fear of failure.

- Someone who shares a story that includes his or her children or enjoyment in spending time with family on the weekends may have values such as family, balance, and flexibility.

- Someone who uses a lot of visual imagery when telling a story (paints a picture in your mind) is likely to be a visual learner.

These bits of knowledge help the coach to assess gaps more clearly, and they become the basis for making individualized hypotheses that can be applied to coaching situations. Note that a hypothesis is different from an assumption because the goal is to affirm or refute it by asking questions.

For example, your employee, Larry, is job shadowing with his co-worker Lucinda to learn how to execute the tasks of his new job. Because he is a visual learner, he needs to receive instructions in a different way from Lucinda (who is not a visual learner). Larry is really struggling to grasp some key elements of the job. He and Lucinda are both becoming frustrated and you are starting to wonder whether you made the right hiring decision. If initially you had asked Larry how he learns best, how he has learned new things in the past, or what would help him to learn his job better, he may have given you clues that would have allowed you to avoid this gap altogether! Instead, you set Larry up to fail because you have partnered him with someone who has an opposite style and who doesn't know how to train him in the way that he learns best.

The point is that you can't close a gap until you know what you are dealing with, and until you elicit the kind of dialog that story telling allows for, you may be missing out on some clues that would help the PBC. The best outcome of story telling happens when the PBC understands his or her own situation more clearly just because it has been verbalized. Many ah-ha moments come during "story time."

Story telling is often as easy as asking the PBC to tell you more about something she just mentioned or about the topic at hand. Have the PBC tell his stories by saying:

- "Tell me more."
- "What can you share?"
- "What is preventing you from reaching your goal, achieving your ideal . . .?"
- "What's going on?"

- "I'd love to hear more about that!"
- "I'd like to hear what you think."
- "How does that impact you?"
- "What are your concerns?"
- "Sounds like you are a bit uncomfortable. Tell me more."
- "How do you feel about that?"
- "What are you struggling with?"
- "Is there something more that you would like to share?"
- "Please, go on. . . ."

If you are a skeptic, we encourage, in fact we dare you, to test this theory of story telling. The next time you are on the bus or a plane, strike up a conversation with a stranger. Practice this skill by encouraging that person to tell you a story by using some of the following statements:

- "That sounds interesting." (Pause)
- "Where are your travels taking you?"
- "Hmmm . . . sounds like a story in there somewhere."
- "Tell me about your [house, kids, pets, job . . .]" (Tap into whatever the person mentioned as a natural part of the conversation.)
- "Wow! That sounds like a great story. I'd love to hear it."

When you try this, make sure you have the time and mental energy to hear what the person has to say, because he or she will tell you! After the stranger has shared the story, take a moment and see how much you now know about him or her . Can you guess his or her values? Joys? Needs? Wants? Challenges? Strengths? What's missing in his or her life? What is he or she striving for? What are the gaps?

Instead of thinking of a story to share back, show more interest, dig deeper into the story by asking open-ended questions that keep the person talking. This is good practice for learning to stay focused on the conversation and learning how to pick up clues that you would dive into if you were conducting a coaching conversation.

How many times in the last twenty-four hours have you talked with someone and felt as though you had his or her undivided attention? In how many of these conversations did you provide your undivided attention, focusing only on the person's message? How much do you avoid soliciting stories because of time or other concerns? When you give someone the opportunity to be heard in the manner presented here, it can do wonders for the relationship and the information exchange. Think about what it would do for you if you were the PBC and somebody was genuinely interested in your story and hanging on your every word.

There are times when it is appropriate for coaches to share *small* pieces of their own stories. But the purpose behind doing this should only be to make a connection with the PBC, not to take over the story telling session. This self-disclosure is for the purpose of disclosing pieces of information about yourself that allow the PBC to relate to you in some way, improve trust, or become unstuck in his or her own thinking. Self-disclosure may suggest that you have been in the person's shoes or that you understand a feeling or emotion because you have experienced it in a similar situation. It is a way of connecting with the person you are coaching. Such statements, if they are brief and relevant, tend to encourage others to feel that they are talking to someone who can identify with their problem. This kind of interaction makes PBCs more open to sharing what's really on their minds.

Coaches must be very careful when telling their stories or providing any self-disclosure when in the *coach role*—not because there is a risk of sharing too much of yourself, but because there is a risk of not knowing when enough is enough! Be careful not to take over the conversation.

Encourage

Challenge
Listen
Encourage
Ask
Refine

Encourage is all about making PBCs feel good about themselves and recognizing their emotions, feelings, and accomplishments. It is about moving people forward and about giving them a reason to continue to make progress toward their goals. It is an essential part of coaching because it validates their feelings and emotions and enhances esteem and confidence. Encourage can be accomplished through making *validate* and *celebrate* statements.

The Encourage skill builds on other skills by making the coaching conversation personal and individualized. It is the job of the coach to validate a PBCs' emotions and feelings as well as keep him or her on the right track, moving forward appropriately and succeeding. As much as the coach plays the role of truth-sayer or reality check person and occasionally devil's advocate, in many ways, the coach is also a PBC's biggest cheerleader and supporter. In the case of executive or senior level leaders, the coach may be one of the few people who provide recognition and encouragement to them.

Think of a time in your past when you have done your best and it went unnoticed. How did it make you feel? On the other hand, think of a time in your life when you were trying or struggling to accomplish something and someone gave you a much-needed pat on the back—not for reaching the goal, but for making the effort to get there. This is what Encourage is about, building esteem and reinforcing strengths!

In Chapter 1, we presented the four conditions for building commitment: being clear, having influence, being competent, and feeling appreciated. Encourage is the skill that reinforces competency and provides expressed appreciation.

As part of building trust and maintaining it throughout the coaching conversation, recognize PBCs for their insights, emotions, and feelings and reward them for their successes, ideas, efforts, and ah-ha moments. Do this by validating the feelings and emotions they are expressing or the insights they come up with, and by recognizing the hard work they just completed by celebrating their accomplishments, building on their strengths, and sharing your feelings about their progress.

Validate Feelings and Emotions

You will be well served by validating, acknowledging, and addressing feelings and emotions in your coaching interactions. People find interactions with others fully satisfying only when they come to believe that they are accepted for what they are feeling and have some sense of what the feelings mean. A large portion of root causes in coaching conversations can be traced back to basic human emotions. Coaches do not have to be touchy-feely, but it is each coach's responsibility to *validate* and acknowledge feelings and emotions.

If a PBC uses any of the words listed below during a coaching conversation, take pause and discuss them. This is only a partial list. It doesn't matter where or how these words are used or in what context within the coaching conversation, when you hear one of them, acknowledge it or ask about it so the PBC has an opportunity to explore further. Remember, there are *positive* feelings and emotions that should be acknowledged, too.

Amazed	Stressed	Hate	Disappointed	Don't care
Happy	Sad	Anticipating	Confident	Confused
Anxious	Feel	Hopeful	Afraid	Excited
Annoyed	Thrilled	Relieved	Believe	Trust/Don't Trust
Angry	Worried	Surprised	Concerned	Frustrated

Whatever you do, when addressing feelings, don't shut the PBC down by saying something like:

- "Oh, Mary, everyone feels that way."

- "Don't get so angry, Herb."
- "There is no reason for you to be upset, Rowena."
- "Lloyd, don't you think you're overreacting just a little?"
- "Maybe you should come back when you can be reasonable, Cort."
- "Can't you be a little more professional, Lorraine?"
- "Calm down, Margaret."

Instead, validate how the PBC feels and give him or her a chance to talk about it. People have a need to share good things and vent about bad things.

Ask about emotions, especially if the PBC is not able to label the feeling initially. Following are some ways to validate feelings and emotions in a skillful manner and keep the PBC moving forward.

- "You mentioned you were angry. What is making you so angry?"
- "You said 'hopeful'; what do you mean by that?"
- "Your disappointment is coming through loud and clear. What are you really thinking?"
- "You sound optimistic and re-energized. Is there anything else you'd like to share?"
- "What are you afraid of?"
- "What would you do if you were not afraid?"
- "What's preventing you from being able to . . .?"
- "What is preventing you from getting what you want?"
- "I can tell that this is really bothering you."
- "Thank you for sharing that. I can tell it was difficult."
- "You seem re-energized already."

One of the biggest pitfalls coaches make is to avoid discussing underlying emotional causes for behaviors or inaction. Sometime we do this because of our own discomfort in dealing with fellings. Moving straight to the tactical (how to fix the issue) when a PBC identifies that he or she is also common, and *afraid* of something is also common, and counterproductive. Dwelling on the tactical means you only focus on the specifics of what is being said, the details of the situation, or solely on the ultimate goal, without regard for the PBC's feelings about such things. The payoff from this kind of conversation is, at best, short-term improvement without long-term results. When a PBC mentions an emotion or touches on a feeling, such as fear, you need to address or explore the fear before going any further. If the emotion isn't overt, use your intuition and ask the PBC about what you are hearing or picking up on an emotional level. See the following example.

Theresa is coming to D'Andrea (her coach) for some moral support about some nervousness she is feeling in her new position.

PBC/THERESA: "Hey, D'Andrea, I need to talk with you about some anxiety I am feeling over this new role I am taking on."

COACH/D'ANDREA: "What's the problem, Theresa? You're perfect for this new role. Besides, everyone is counting on you!"

PBC/THERESA: "Yeah, that's what I hear, on both counts. But, no pressure, right?"

COACH/D'ANDREA: "You know you've got what it takes, you're just having first week jitters."

PBC/THERESA: "You think so? I don't know. . . ."

COACH/D'ANDREA: "I know so. Now how are you going to wow them at that meeting on Monday?"

Theresa may perform well at the meeting on Monday, but what about after that? Her real concerns, her emotions, were never addressed. This example also shows that encouragement for encouragement sake is also ineffective.

To deal with emotions, don't avoid, pull yourself out of the detail and focus on the emotions that you hear, see, or intuit coming from the PBC, and ask the person to share more. If D'Andrea were to do things differently and address what Theresa was feeling, she could have said something like: "Theresa, taking on a new role is always a bit daunting. What is it that is creating so much anxiety for you?"

The following is another example of a potential coaching disaster that occurred during a coaching workshop practice session. This example illustrates how important it is to address the emotional component before trying to solve the problem.

The issue was that the PBC (a trainer named Dakota) was going against protocol (after new-hire training was complete) by giving new employees answers to questions instead of referring them back to their managers for questions about the job and how to find much-needed resources. The impact was that Dakota was not always getting her work done due to becoming the "go to" person, and the managers were not getting a clear picture of how these new employees were challenged in order to provide additional direction and training on the job, all of which led to some serious problems in productivity and communication. Lila, the coach, brings the *why* to the table in this conversation.

COACH/LILA: "Dakota, I've noticed you are spending a lot of time working with the employees who just graduated from training. How is that impacting your productivity?"

PBC/DAKOTA: "Well, I suppose it takes a little time out of my day, but it's no big deal, I enjoy helping them."

COACH/LILA: "What kinds of things are you helping them with?"

PBC/DAKOTA: "All kinds of things, Lila. You know they always have questions about how to do this or that, or where to find certain procedures."

COACH/LILA: "Aren't those things their managers could help them with?"

PBC/DAKOTA: "Sometimes, but I don't think they always get the right answer, and then they come to me anyway. I'm okay with it. Besides, the managers are so busy. Honestly, I don't know that I always trust the managers to give them all the information they need, and besides, I am more available."

COACH/LILA: "I know that helping the new hires is important to you. Unfortunately, Dakota, playing the expert to the new employees is taking more than a little time out of your day, and it is affecting your personal productivity for the work that's assigned to you. Since it isn't part of your scope to do all this extra work, I have to ask you, How can you make it so you are less available to these new hires?"

PBC/DAKOTA: "Well, if I can't help them, who will?"

COACH/LILA: "It is a part of their manager's job."

PBC/DAKOTA: "Well, what if they don't help them?"

The coach, Lila, chose to ignore the expressed feeling/emotion—*trust* or more appropriately, *mistrust*—the first time it was brought up and moved directly to finding a solution to the problem. Note that Dakota, the PBC, did not always use the word "trust." Some of the mistrust was implied by other words that she used, another reason why it is important to explore the feelings to be sure of what you are hearing. Because this coach moved to the tactical and continued to ask questions like, "How can you direct these employees elsewhere to get their questions answered?" and "What can you do to make it so they don't take up all your time asking you these questions, so you can still get your work done?" she and Dakota went round and round for another fifteen minutes, and the "trust" issue came up another two or three times.

Ultimately, Lila missed (or avoided) the root cause of the problem. Therefore, even though Dakota might begin sending new employees back to their managers, chances are the behavior won't last. Without exploring the root cause (trust), Dakota is not going to be committed to changing her behaviors long-term. This type of conversation not only sets her up to fail, but it sets the coach up for frustration. It also means that this is not the last time the topic will be addressed between these two. It's not that Dakota doesn't know *how* to send the new employees elsewhere, or that she couldn't put a stop to the distractions, it's that she didn't trust who she was sending them to.

If this situation had been handled differently, it is likely that one conversation would take care of the problem. When given a do-over, the coach addressed the real problem by coming up with the following questions:

- "You implied you don't trust the managers to give their employees the right answers. Tell me more about that."

- "I heard you say you don't trust the managers. Where do you think that comes from?"

- "Is there anything you can do to feel more comfortable with trusting the managers to deal with their own employees so that you can concentrate on your work?"

- "How can you influence the managers to provide the right answers so that you don't have to?"

Can you see how these questions differ from the previous tactical ones?

Once the trust issue was fully explored, another layer was discovered by the PBC. Dakota believed herself to be in a position of helpfulness and authority with the new employees. She also thought that since she had been a part of the new hires' initial training that she was responsible for making them successful (she had unclear expectations of her role). It wasn't so much about whether the managers would have an answer for the new hires but whether they would have the "right" answers—in this case, the "right" answer was one that Dakota thought only she could provide. The PBC did not want to let go of her control for starters, and she didn't want to lose her designation as the "go to" person, which fed her self-esteem. She didn't want the new hires to fail and she didn't *trust* the others to do a good enough job in providing important information because they were so busy. Once all of this was realized, the coaching conversation progressed nicely and included actions the PBC could take in order to relinquish some of the control back to the managers and still be peripherally involved with the new hires' success. Moral of the story: when it comes to feelings and emotions, go there!

In corporate America, as well as many other settings, addressing, let alone validating and acknowledging, feelings and emotions has become somewhat of a taboo. Whether it is because people have politically corrected themselves into a corner, see expressing and addressing feelings as a sign of weakness, or simply aren't comfortable dealing with the "personal stuff," the last thing some coaches want to do is spend time dealing with feelings and emotions! If you haven't heard it before now, let us be the first to tell you, it is time well spent! Getting to a root cause of an issue only happens if you validate the PBC feelings and emotions.

Celebrate

Celebrate is another way to Encourage the PBC and should be ongoing throughout the coaching conversation. *Celebrate* by recognizing the PBC. The misconception is that celebration has to be some type of ticker-tape parade that announces stellar performance to the world or that it should be a gushing display of gratitude. Not true. It can be as simple as a "Thank you for a job well done," "I'm proud of you," or "You did a lot of work here." These are valid statements even if the task is part of the job.

Whenever a PBC makes an incremental improvement such as accomplishing an action item, trying something different, making a successful behavior change, or any step in the right direction, celebration is in order. Old habits cannot be broken; they must be replaced with new habits or behaviors. If there is no positive reinforcement to this new way of doing things, what is the point? People repeat behaviors that are rewarded. They need a sense of payoff. Some sort of return on their investment. It is your job to help them recognize their successes and provide some return for their investment.

At first, it may be hard for you to see beyond your own biases to choose to celebrate incremental improvement on behalf of the PBC. We hope that you will eventually see the payoff to this kind of action with improved performance and added commitment to goals. Please remember to always be sincere and specific in making your celebratory comments; it maintains trust.

Celebrate Statements

- "Congratulations on not taking over the meeting from your team member this time. I know that you are focusing on not micromanaging your team as part of your action plan. This is a personal success for you!"

- "Your ability to engage others is quite good. It made a big impact in today's meeting because you made everyone feel heard."

- "Your input at today's meeting was of great value to solving our distribution problem."

- "How can you celebrate the fact that you have accomplished [specify goal]?"

- "Let's take a moment to discuss how your success regarding your communication strategy impacts your goals."

Now it's your turn. What celebrate statements can you think of? (Additional validate and celebrate statements are included in Appendix C.)

Ask

Challenge
Listen
Encourage
Ask
Refine

If you are successful in your job, it is safe to assume that you didn't get to where you are today without being an expert in what you do. Often in coaching conversations, expertise can be an impediment to the coach's ability to Ask probing and open-ended questions without leading the PBC. When you know so much, you are more likely to want to share your experience, opinions, knowledge, and what has worked for you. Ultimately, you want others to learn from *your* mistakes. It is important to recognize that you probably would not have become the expert you are if someone had not allowed you to make your own mistakes. Thus, for successful implementation of the Ask skill, we ask that you shift to that *egoless* perspective and leave your biases and expertise at the door. Otherwise, you may have an inclination or desire to solve for PBCs or lead them to "your way" of thinking.

Ask is about leading PBCs to *their* way of thinking. Coaches do this by asking questions—not just any questions, but ones that are probing, compelling, thought-provoking, pivotal, curious, allow for great latitude in response, and allow the PBC to discover how to achieve his or her ideal state. These are *coaching questions*.

Coaching Questions

Coaching questions show you are interested in the PBC and the coaching conversation. *Coaching questions* are those that make the PBC think. They are searching and open-ended and do not restrict the respondent to one- or two-word answers, nor do they restrict by implying the opinions or biases of the coach. Coaching questions allow people to process information verbally and make connections. They promote thought for those who need to process information internally. When a PBC responds to a coaching question, it assists the coach in achieving clearer understanding of where the PBCs is, and guides the coach in knowing where to go next in the coaching conversation. For PBCs, coaching questions assist them in figuring out their own solutions and actions.

Asking coaching questions allows PBCs to figure out *what* needs to happen and *how* they will achieve it, *what* they are willing to commit to, and *how* they need to behave to obtain the desired results.

Getting good at asking coaching questions from an *egoless* perspective requires practice for most people. Questions that garner a one-word response, lead a PBC down a particular path (possibly yours), or overall do not promote independent thought from the PBC, are not coaching questions.

The purpose of all coaching questions is to find out information. The use of open-ended questions is like going fishing with a net. You catch a number of fish. Closed-ended questions, which only allow for a "yes," "no," or one-word answers are like fishing with a hook. You are only going to catch one fish at a time. Which is fine if you are okay with throwing each fish back (having multiple conversations about the same topic) until you get the one that you want! A good rule of thumb to follow is, if you are at a point in a coaching conversation where you are trying to gather more information from the PBC, then coaching questions will help you do that. If you are trying to clarify or test for concurrence, then a few closed questions can be useful. Keep in mind that when several closed questions are strung together, without any time for the PBC to elaborate, your conversation may sound like an interrogation. This may cause the PBC to become passive or detach from the conversation. What is worse is that, besides not knowing which question to answer first, the PBC may respond only based on what he or she thinks you want to hear.

One way to practice the Ask skill is to pay attention to how often you ask closed questions during a conversation. How often do you make statements that assume you and the PBC are thinking alike? Are there any questions that you ask regularly that could be made more like coaching questions by opening them up (try adding a "what" or a "how" before the question)? How often do you begin a question with "Have you thought of . . .?" which is a leading question designed to move PBCs in your direction, not theirs.

How to Create and Ask Coaching Questions

You can use the following tips to help you create and Ask your own coaching questions:

- The best coaching questions are created when you are *not* focused on trying to be perfect. There is no such thing as the perfect question! If you Listen and remain objective, the right questions will come to you at the right times.

- It is *not* imperative that you think of a question immediately after the PBC stops talking. You can have process time (refer back to *benefits of* silence in the Listen skill section).

- Ask questions that start with "what" and "how." They are the most powerful.

- What have you tried?
- What do you need from them?
- How do you know?
- What is the ideal?
- How can you make it happen?

- "Why" questions are *only* appropriate if you ensure they do not imply blame or put the PBC on the defensive. Sometimes adding a phrase before the why can be helpful. Choose your tone of voice carefully when asking "why" questions. You can also add "what" to a "why" question in some cases. For example, "What are the reasons why you are hesitating?" This does not imply blame; rather it probes further.

- Avoid questions that lead the PBC in one direction or the other: "Have you thought of . . .?" "Did you try . . .?" "Would it be helpful for you to . . .?" and, "Do you think you could . . .?" These kinds of questions communicate that there is a right and wrong way to do something and that the right way is usually your way.

- Keep questions short, succinct, and clear.

- Ask one question at a time. Do not rapidly fire several questions at once—especially if each question limits the answer. This diminishes the power of the first question exponentially, and it may indicate that you are trying to direct the PBC to a solution that you have in your head.

- Remain *egoless*.

- Pretend you are not the expert (even if you are).

- Be aware of your tone.

- Only ask if you are willing to hear the other person's answer!

- Avoid statements that impose bias.

- If you are unclear, ask more questions.

- Questions should not be a means of telling. If you have something to say, say it.

- Allow the PBC to answer your coaching questions without interruption.

- When it comes to legal or compliance issues, don't ask unless there is room for flexibility and autonomy on the part of the PBC. Save your time and theirs by stating what the parameters are and then ask questions about how the PBC can work within the rules or be creative *within* the box.

Flash back to the InDiCom coaching model. The majority of your coaching questions will be more about exploring options versus finding solutions. Be willing to ask a lot of questions that are discovery-oriented rather than solution-oriented.

A list Thirty-Five Coaching Questions can be found Appendix A.

The purpose of asking coaching questions is to keep the conversation moving in a targeted manner and to encourage the PBC to do most of the talking. Another way to accomplish this is to replace questions with *powerful statements* or "verbal nodding." Powerful statements and verbal nodding are implied questions or encouraging behaviors that allow PBCs to monologue similarly to how they would when asked a coaching question.

Sample Powerful Statements and Verbal Nodding

- "Tell me more about that."

- "Really." (Pause)

- "Let's hear the latest."

- "I've gotten conflicting reports."

- "I've heard good things." (Pause)

- "Sounds like a story."

- "I'm listening." (Be careful with your tone on this one!)

- "Go on."

- "Please continue."

- "uh huh."

- "mmmm."

- "I see."

- "Okay."

- "Yes."

- "Right."

- "I understand."

- "Yes, I follow that."

- "Oh yes, I see where you are going."

Powerful statements and verbal nodding are *not* the same as reality checks and requests. They are statements used in place of coaching questions. They are what you use to keep the coaching conversation flowing.

Refine

Challenge
Listen
Encourage
Ask
Refine

Refine is the skill that keeps the coaching conversation on topic, on track, and relevant. Refine is about not letting the PBC try to fix other people, but rather having the PBC focus on his or her part in the situation and what he or she can do about it. In other words, what is the PBC's role?

The Refine skill is about making sure that the coaching conversation is primarily unidirectional in nature. Not that the dialog won't have its twists, turns, and even backward glances, but ultimately it should move the PBC forward to action.

During a coaching conversation, a number of things can occur that prevent the conversation from progressing in a positive direction. The PBC may do any of the following:

- Blame others for his or her circumstances.

- Have outbursts of strong emotions such as anger, hostility, fear, or anxiety.

- Shut down; make little or no verbal response and not participate fully in the interaction.

- Begin to cover the same ground over and over again.

- Be surprised by the topic and need preparation time to discuss it.

- Become too tired or distracted to engage further in the conversation.

There is some need for immediacy in working with the Refine skill. Immediacy meaning that the coach must be able to respond to "real time" conditions, such as those listed above. Refine includes focusing the coaching conversation on the here and now. It includes making statements that draw attention to the things that sidetrack or block the progress of the coaching session and being open to strategies that can overcome these obstacles or distractions. Sample statements may include:

- "A moment ago we were talking about your difficult employee. I notice we're now talking about something else. Would you like to go back to the employee situation first or stay with this topic?"

- "I recall you saying something about your boss. Now you're talking about how much you hate to be controlled by anyone. Help me to understand what this has to do with the original conversation about your boss."

- "I can tell that you are upset. Would you like a moment to recollect your thoughts before we continue?"

- "I can see that you are really keeping an eye on your watch.
  Would you prefer we have this conversation at a different time?"

Refining the conversation can be necessary for a variety of reasons. There may be times during the coaching conversation when it seems as if you are going nowhere fast. Perhaps the PBC has digressed away from the topic and continues to ramble on about things irrelevant to the conversation. This kind of monologue or venting can prevent getting to the point and take the focus of the conversation completely off track.

Perhaps the PBC is doing what we call *dodging*, which means he or she has intentionally or unintentionally taken you off topic to avoid the subject. Recognizing the "art of the dodge" can be useful as a coach. *Dodging* is something that people do when the conversation becomes uncomfortable for one reason or another. People may dodge to end a conversation quickly or because they do not want to, or are not ready to address certain behaviors, patterns, or emotions. PBCs may dodge by agreeing too quickly, turning questions back to the coach, or lead the coach down a different path just to get the conversation off track. They may also dodge by placing blame or playing the victim role in order to divert attention from themselves. People don't always dodge on purpose; it can be subconscious. Sometimes dodging is hard to recognize. Using the Listen skill in these cases can be helpful. When you hear it, redirect the conversation back to the main topic.

Refining the conversation is much easier when coaches are willing to be direct and specific and when they are willing to jump in before things get too far out of hand. Be reasonable in your redirection and allow for *some* digression and discussion that is off topic. Simply be aware of when use of the Refine skill is needed, and when you see the need to bring the conversation back to the point. Following are some common examples of Refine:

Refine Samples

- Redirect by validating concerns/feelings without allowing the divergent topic to take over the conversation. Then restate the goal or the objective:

"Brandon, I can see that discussing your success is making you uncomfortable. We all need recognition from time to time, and I can assure you that this is not a way of getting you to do more work. I simply think you are ready for the next level if you want to go there."

- Politely stop the divergent conversation and redirect to the specific outcomes you have agreed on or reiterate the ideal state:

"Excuse me, Mary Ann? I can appreciate that you have a complex life outside of work. As your coach, I am concerned about your life here at work. How can you focus on you and your sales numbers right now?"

- Ask the PBC to focus on the solution, not the problem:

"Cila, you are not being blamed or criticized. I simply need your help in solving this issue so that there is a positive outcome for everyone."

- Ask the PBC to focus on him- or herself, not the part or responsibility of others:

"Terri, I appreciate your input and understand your feelings. Right now we are talking about you. How can you improve your partnering skills?"

- Find out what the PBC has influence (if not control) over in the situation:

"Rose, what pieces of the project *can* you influence?"

- Explore what the PBC can own:

"Jeff, what three things can you commit to at this time?"

- Reassure the PBC that you have his or her best interest at heart and that your role is to help:

"Alan, I want to assure you that I am interested in your success, and part of my role as your coach is to point out any obstacles that might impede that success."

- Call out the behavior or the (suspected) emotion and ask where the PBC would like to go from here:

  - "What are you avoiding?" (pause for response) "What would you like to do about it?"

As for PBCs, your role is to make sure they are taking ownership of their behaviors, actions, and scope of influence. If you find that a PBC is not taking ownership or starts to place blame, find helpful ways to get the PBC back on track and focused on what he or she can influence or control.

If a PBC continues to cite chapter and verse as to why the current situation is not his or her fault or beyond his or her control, try something like the following:

- "What *is* within your scope of influence, Paula?"

- "Right now, we are discussing *your* behavior, Shirley."

- "Why don't we focus on *you* right now, Anna."

- "What needs to happen in order for *you* to take accountability for your actions in this situation, Pat?"

- "What is one thing you can do, Kristin?"

- "What would *you* like for this situation to look like, Vince? How can you make that a reality?"

Two-Words

Two-Words, or the *Two-Word technique,* is a way of having PBCs gain clarity about the gap and Refine where they are and where they want to go. Two-Words simply has you ask *two* specific coaching questions in succession:

Current Reality: "What **one word** best describes where you are, right now, with your situation?" Allow the PBC to come up with his or her own word (words or phrases are okay, too).

Ideal State: "Now, what **one word** would best describe what you want it to be, or your ideal?" Allow the PBC to answer.

Putting the PBC's Two-Words together, in a "From/To" format helps identify the gap and gives a PBC a means to move forward.

- "How are you going to go from _____ to _____?" (Use the PBC's words.)
- "What is one thing can you do to move from *overwhelmed* to *relief*?"

Sample Two-Word Responses from PBCs
From:

- Outcast to Accepted
- Busy to Purposeful
- Driven to Effective
- Sledge Hammer to Rubber Mallet
- Tired to Energized
- Aggressive to Coach
- Expert to Coach
- Challenged to Easy
- Authoritative to Friend
- Criticized to Freedom
- Fearful to Free

This technique helps the PBC see clearly where he or she is "currently" and where he or she "wants to be." Thus the PBC should now be able to see how big the gap is between his or her current reality and his or her ideal state. Is it a huge gap that needs to be broken down into smaller pieces, or is it a small gap that only requires a minor tweak in behavior or plan of action on the part of the PBC?

Two-Words can be used at any stage of the coaching model. When used at the Involve stage, it will help clarify the purpose; at the Discover stage, it gives clarity to the size of the gap; in the Commit stage, it summarizes the PBC's action plan into two simple words. The words can also be used to open future coaching conversations:

- "Jourdan, last time we talked you said you were *apprehensive* about the interview, and you wanted to be more *comfortable* with it. Where are you right now?"
- "Tanner, how are you doing at going from *expert* to *coach* with your employees?"

The benefit of this technique to the coach is that you now get to use these words as a point of reference in your coaching conversation. And speaking the PBC's language helps build and maintain trust and create common ground.

As you become more comfortable with this technique, use the Two-Words that PBCs provide to assist them in finding solutions, creating ah-ha moments, and gaining commitment to their plans of action.

Metaphors

We find that the final technique, *metaphors,* is the most advanced technique a coach can master. Metaphors are an effective way to put a situation or issue into a context the PBC can better understand. Metaphors allow PBCs to relate their current situations to something that they already have expertise in or knowledge about. A metaphor is a figure of speech, symbol, or image that can help illustrate a point and connect similar or dissimilar items. A PBC who has no idea how to go about tackling a large project can use a metaphor to help get his or her arms around the project.

To use a metaphor, simply listen for clues, like being involved in sports, or having children, and see whether the PBC's knowledge in one area can be transferred to the coaching topic.

Sample Metaphors from the Coach

If you know the PBC well, you can often use what you know about the person to create a metaphor.

- "Bob, compare this to not being able to be on the soccer field, playing the game *for* your kids?"

- "Heidi, compare this to putting together a 5,000-piece jigsaw puzzle?" (build the frame first, then complete the large center point object, then work on the detail)

Sometimes it's easier for PBCs to come up with their own metaphors. You can help by asking questions:

- "Is there anything else in your life that you can compare this to?"
- "When have you been in a similar situation?"
- "When have you felt this way before?"
- "Is there a way for you to connect this to something you already know, are good at, etc. . . . ."
- "Is there any other challenging time in your life that you came through well?"

Once the PBC has answered, find ways to compare the answers with what he or she is dealing with now.

When people are able to see how to apply familiar processes and behaviors or attach their situations to prior knowledge, it makes it easier for them to come up with action plans. It also enhances esteem and gives them confidence. Using metaphors can be a tremendous tool for moving PBCs forward. Typically, PBCs know they need to do something (*what*). They just don't know *how* to start. Common metaphors that can be used in coaching include:

- Sports
- Games
- Scrapbooking
- Gardening
- Parenting
- Objects ("I feel like a ship adrift at sea.")
- Learning to drive a car

- TV/movies
- Major purchase decisions (can apply same process to making a career decision)
- Spirit/Religion

Metaphors are a way to connect images, descriptions of everyday things, previous experiences, or applications of prior knowledge with the present situation. As the coach, you are welcome to help the PBC come up with a metaphor. If you really want to challenge yourself, learn how to have the PBC come up with his or her own metaphors by asking pivotal coaching questions. Regardless of who identifies the metaphor, coach or PBC, the goal is to use them to help the PBC make connections to move forward.

The following are two examples of the metaphor technique:

Sample 1

PBC/TOM: "I just don't know what I want out of my next job. I don't know what kind of company I want to work for. I don't think I want to be in the same industry. Ora, how do I choose a new job or figure out what companies I even want to apply to?"

COACH/ORA: "I can tell, Tom, that you are really struggling with this. Looking for a new job is a lot like making a major purchase. There is a lot at stake! What types of major purchases have you made in the last year or two?"

PBC/TOM: "Well, I bought a car."

COACH/ORA: "Great, Tom, walk me through the steps of how you decided what car to buy."

PBC/TOM: "Well, Ora, I wanted something reliable that would last a long time, good gas mileage was important, something not too expensive. I wanted certain amenities and I was willing to settle for fewer features, but only if it meant that the price was right. Then I researched to find a reputable dealer. . . ."

COACH/ORA: "It sounds like you did a great job picking out your car and you did your homework! Tom, if you were to think in terms of the process you used in buying your car and apply it to your job search, what would it look like?"

Sample 2

COACH/DAWN: ". . . Thank you for sharing that, Gino. I agree that it is important for you to stop micromanaging your employees if you want them to stop being so dependent on you."

PBC/GINO: "But how, Dawn? I am so used to doing it!"

COACH/DAWN: "Let's use a metaphor to help you work through this. Think about a time when your kids had to do something for themselves and you could not interfere."

PBC/GINO: "My oldest daughter, Debbie, is on the soccer team. Every game I go to I have to restrain myself from running out on the field and showing her where she should be standing or yelling commands to her on how to win. My wife, Jasmine, has to restrain me every time. From my perspective in the stands, I can see the moves that the opponent is about to take and I want to warn her, protect her. Of course, she has a soccer coach for that and I know I need to respect that, but it's really hard to just be a fan. Plus, what would she learn if Daddy were always coming to her rescue?"

COACH/DAWN: "How do you think your daughter would feel if you did run out on the field?"

PBC/GINO: "Are you kidding, I would be banned from her games for life, and she'd hate me."

COACH/DAWN: "Yet, from what you've said, you're behaving that way with your direct reports at work."

PBC/GINO: "Hmm, hadn't thought of it that way before."

COACH/DAWN: "How can you apply some of this same restraint you use at the soccer games with your desire to interfere less with your team?"

Using a metaphor is a great way to create ah-ha moments and move the PBC forward.

As a whole, using the CLEAR coaching skills in conjunction with the InDiCom coaching model is a surefire recipe for your coaching success!

Coaching Moment

Current Reality: Which of the CLEAR coaching skills do you think you are most proficient at?

Ideal State: Which ones do you want to improve your ability to use and incorporate into your coaching conversations? If you took the CSI, what was your coaching skills gap?

Action Plan: Identify one skill that you may not have used before or would like to focus on mastering. How can you begin to accomplish that goal?

Chapter Summary

This chapter presented the CLEAR coaching skills that are to be used in conjunction with the InDiCom coaching model.

Challenge

- Challenge means a coach relies on *intuition* to follow the conversation and really pay attention to what is happening with the PBC. Use intuition to identify when to deliver a *request* or a *reality check*.

Listen

- Listen means that you listen for more than what is being said, understand the benefits of *silence*, encourage *story telling* on the part of the PBC, and use limited self-disclosure in order to give the PBC center stage.

Encourage

- Encourage is all about making the PBC feel good about and recognizing his or her feelings, emotions, and accomplishments,

which gives a reason to continue moving forward. It includes
statements that *validate* and *celebrate.*

Ask

* *Ask* coaching questions that are pivotal and thought-provoking
  as well as open-ended and probing. Use *powerful statements* and
  verbal nodding in conjunction with coaching questions when
  there is more to discover (for example, "Tell me more . . .").

Refine

* Refine means that the coach continually keeps the coaching
  conversation on track and using techniques such as *Two-Words*
  and *metaphors.*

7

Plan to Coach

"A goal without a plan is just a wish."

—Larry Elder

THE *COACH ROLE* is commonly used by managers when they conduct one-on-ones or need to have a performance coaching conversation with a team member. Ideally, during one-on-ones, the PBC brings anything he or she wants to discuss to the manager. It is the team member's time to share accomplishments, challenges, or successes. Performance coaching, on the other hand, is usually initiated by the manager, who brings an issue or problem (the *why*) to the attention of a team member. Knowing how to present the issue to the employee and then shift to the *coach role* takes concentrated effort and planning.

All coaches, even the most seasoned ones, do some pre-planning. If they are addressing a performance problem, they plan for how to approach the situation. This type of planning is ongoing in that it occurs before every performance coaching conversation. Note-taking is another type of planning. Coaches typically decide up-front whether they are going to take notes during their coaching conversations. This way they can obtain the PBC's permission or acknowledgement at the onset. Another type of planning that occurs is to determine how coaching conversations will be conducted. Will they be in person (face-to-face) or virtual (phone, email, video conference)? And finally, if the coach intends to shadow the PBC (follow and observe the PBC in a day-to-day setting) or use 360-degree feedback as a coaching tool, planning is a must. Each of these types of planning is presented in this chapter.

Performance Coaching

To begin, let's take a look at the more difficult coaching conversations you will encounter and how some advanced planning on your part can turn them into fruitful conversations. A performance coaching conversation is defined as one during which you, the coach, confront someone with an issue or problem that needs to be solved. The key point here is that the coach is the one initiating the coaching conversation and the conversation has a clear purpose. The coach has something in mind that needs to be addressed or fixed. In essence, the coach is the one communicating the *why*. (*Why* are we having this coaching conversation?)

Each time coaches confront people, especially with a performance issue, they introduce the possibility of change. Each time they introduce change, they introduce the possibility of resistance. When you communicate the *why*, you accept the responsibility for managing the resistance that you create. Dealing with defensive reactions is something you will need to learn how to do. (A sample performance coaching conversation can be found in Chapter 8.)

Coaches can prepare themselves for performance coaching conversations and for dealing with resistance and negative emotions by being clear with the PBC about the *why* of the conversation up front, knowing how to reduce resistance, and by focusing on the future. Sometimes it is helpful to plan out what you will say or do in advance.

Being Clear About the Why

Performance coaching conversations require that you take a slightly different approach during the Involve stage of the InDiCom coaching model. Stage I of the InDiCom coaching model (Involve) is about clarifying the purpose and expectations; how you approach this stage differs because you are the one communicating the *why* at the start of the performance coaching conversation.

In the Involve stage, performance issues should be dealt with one at a time. Avoid the laundry list approach. It is counterproductive. Ideally, if you have more than one issue to address, schedule separate conversations.

When presenting the problem, start with the most recent example of the performance issue and be specific. Typically, clarifying the purpose consists of the coach's initial statement of *why* (why are we having this conversation?) that is, what needs to be changed, fixed, or improved.

Clarifying the purpose includes making sure that expectations, objectives, outcomes, results, opportunities, and/or potential are clearly identified and communicated. To accomplish this, precisely state the performance or proficiency gap using specific examples, behaviors, results, or data and identify how the PBC's performance differs from your expectations or established standards. Caution yourself against providing evaluations of attitudes, feelings, and general characteristics that do not directly address the performance issue and avoid making assumptions that you know the cause of the problem. Even when you think you are right, you should never guess about what is going on with another person. Instead you should ask questions that allow PBCs to explain their points of view ("Help me understand what's happening.").

Performance problems have a better chance of being addressed effectively when they are presented in a direct manner and coupled with an *impact statement* that specifies the results of the PBC's behavior.

Sample impact statements are:

- "When you treat customers poorly, we lose the customer and you lesson your chances for the bonus tier."

- "When you come to work late, your teammates have to pick up the slack and it causes overtime."

- "When you don't keep me informed of your project status, I don't know how to convey what you're doing to senior management."

Sometimes the impact statement gets wrapped into the context of describing the gap. This is okay. Just remember that telling the impact is important.

In order for conversations to be productive, begin by identifying the *specific* behavior and its impact. Using statements that are generalizations can diminish the power of coaching and add time to the conversation. If you are not used to being specific in your coaching, you may need to plan ahead and create some of these comments in advance. Use the examples below as a guide.

- Instead of "Karen, you are not a team player" or "Karen, you have a bad attitude," try, "Karen, your use of sarcasm in team meetings violates our team's guiding principles and impacts overall team trust."

- Instead of, "Donyelle, you are very willing and always show a good attitude," which communicates that the person is positively regarded but fails to illuminate the specific behavior that you are trying to reinforce, try, "Donyelle, it really sets a great example for other team members when you stay upbeat during high-volume times," which specifies the positive behavior you want to reinforce.

The following examples address even more specific performance gaps:

- "Hello, Hans. Thanks for coming in to see me today. I have been looking over last week's numbers and I see you fell short of your sales goal by 25 percent. Now, I know that you normally have no trouble reaching your weekly goals; in fact, you are often one of our star performers! Share with me what happened last week."

- "Wendy, I have observed your interactions with your new direct reports and it appears that you are hesitant to take on the leadership role. These people are looking to you to be their leader and provide direction. By not playing that role you could cause more confusion and harm to the team's progress and cohesiveness. Help me understand what's happening."

- "Sophie, it appears that you are trying to control almost every move your employees make. This indicates that you do not trust them. I know you don't want to be perceived this way." (Pause.)

- "Gary, you seem to be struggling with your new expanded role. By not taking action on the projects they asked you to work on, people are wondering if they made the right decision to promote you. Would you like to talk?"

- "Deb, last month we had agreed that every team member would be at the training sessions. I have been to every session this month and I haven't seen you there. By not attending, we will be out of compliance and singled out in the audit report. I'm open to hearing what's going on."

- "Fiona, the travel office policy states that unless there is an emergency, travel requests must be submitted at least forty-eight hours prior to actual travel. I have three memos here from the travel office indicating that you have not been following the rule and it's causing a backlog with other reservations. Share with me what's going on."

"Softening the blow" is a common problem in introducing the *why* in performance coaching conversations. It may save a person's feelings, but could diminish the power of your opening statements. Be wary of starting out with a compliment that leads to a criticism. Even though you may think you are softening the blow, are you really? Take a look at the example below:

COACH: "Heidi, thanks for coming in today. I wanted to let you know how much I appreciate the extra help you gave us with the company picnic last week; *however*, I noticed that because of your dedication to that project, your service levels have now slumped significantly. You have a lot to make up for this week. Have you thought about how you can catch up?"

Starting out with a compliment is fine, as long as it doesn't turn into criticism. Avoid words such as "but," "however," and "on the other hand," which, when used, negate everything that came before. Instead, just use two separate sentences.

COACH: "Heidi, thanks for coming in today. I wanted to let you know how much I appreciate the extra help you gave us with the company picnic last week. I noticed that because of your dedication to that other project last week, your service levels are now behind. It appears you have a lot to make up for this week. Have you thought about how you can catch up?"

Watch your tone in interactions like these. If disappointment or frustration is in your voice, the PBC will hear it and react.

For you to be effective using the *coach role* in performance coaching conversations, the PBC must agree that a performance issue or gap exists. To accomplish this ownership on the part of the PBC, let go of your own definition of the problem and go into the conversation with the mindset of seeking to understand. Turning the issue over to the PBC may result in *you* seeing things differently, too!

When the coaching conversation starts with the coach communicating a *why* that makes the PBC bristle or upset, establishing ownership and agreement becomes more difficult. When you encounter resistance you can easily revert back to your old ways of solving the problem. Instead, we ask you to stay the course. The PBC accepting ownership of the problem depends on your ability to stay in the *coach role*. By doing this, you will greatly enhance the PBC's willingness to agree that a performance issue exists and to overcome or eliminate it.

All too often in coaching workshops and seminars, leaders witness participants (coaches) who are not at all comfortable with the notion of letting go of any part of their own solutions as they practice using the coaching model. Letting go does not mean that you, the coach, should forget why you started a conversation in the first place. This can be one of the more difficult concepts for coaches to master. It is by helping PBCs explore fully their own reactions that you can turn a problem-solving confrontation into a coaching conversation—one that is mutually satisfying and one in which the PBC is fully involved and feels fully respected. Thus, giving each PBC the freedom to present his or her point of view and explore feelings does not negate your purpose. People are more open when they feel they have a part in creating a solution that works for them. Sometimes you will need to accept incremental improvements that put ownership and, ultimately, action back onto the PBC. Part of your planning then becomes, "What am I willing to accept in this situation?" The following is an illustration of this concept.

COACH/SYLVIA: "Lyle, I've noticed that you are not using your scheduled vacation and that, even when you do, you seem to be working at least part of the vacation day from home."

PBC/LYLE: "I know, Sylvia. I've been doing that for years. I have way too much to do and my vacation time seems to be the only time I can get caught up at work."

COACH/SYLVIA: "Even an athlete needs rest to maintain peak performance. By not taking your vacation, Lyle, I'm concerned that you are not performing at your peak and possibly setting yourself up for burnout. You're too valuable of an employee to lose."

PBC/LYLE: "I haven't looked at it that way. I'm going to rethink this vacation stuff. And I wonder if I could start looking at it as a 'to do' item. I don't know why I have this overwhelming need to accomplish so many things every day. Maybe just taking the vacation could be considered my accomplishment on those days. I may need your help to rethink how I view vacation time."

COACH/SYLVIA: "I'd love to help. Where would you like to start?"

In a performance coaching conversation, by the time you leave the Involve stage, you should know the purpose of the coaching conversation (even if it changes from the original purpose), expectations should be clear, and ownership should be established. This requires removing any resistance.

Reducing Resistance

To manage resistance, dispel the negative emotions associated with it. Think of the process this way: by encouraging others to vent and explore their opinions, feelings, points of view, reasons, and excuses, coaches are helping them transform negative energies into words that lead PBCs to discover root causes, especially once you can get them moving forward.

When presenting something that may trigger a reaction, know how to respond to the PBC. This requires discipline. When people are confronted, expect them to react. How you respond to their reaction will make or break your coaching conversation.

Two typical PBC reactions you can anticipate are:

- PBC makes excuses.
- PBC takes offense or attacks.

When the PBC reacts in either of these ways, remain in the *coach role* and Listen. Don't fall into the trap of displaying equally poor behaviors. It is important to know how you should *not* behave.

When the PBC makes excuses, ***do not:***

- Dismiss, refute, or try to disprove.
- Continue to restate the performance issue in a harsher, more abrasive manner.
- Aggravate the negative impact of the issue by quoting policy or giving some other kind of argument.

If the PBC takes offense or attacks, *do not:*

- React to the PBC's aggressive behavior by becoming aggressive.
- Retreat and back off from the confrontation, try to smooth it over, or shut down.

People react for a variety of reasons. Sometimes it is to avoid conflict, sometimes it is to create it, and sometimes the real reason lies somewhere in between. Because feelings and emotions are involved, reactions happen. Regardless of how PBCs react, on some level their reactions are valid because, if they feel it, it is real to them. Thus, the guiding principle in confronting a performance problem is not to fight the person's reaction; instead, understand it and focus on performance and resolution. Use caution in moving forward in your coaching conversation if emotions are still high. If the PBC has not accepted ownership of the problem, chances are the coaching conversation will not be a success. Get the PBC to talk! Allow him or her to vent for a short time, and then move forward. Use some of the CLEAR coaching skills to assist with resistance you may encounter.

Try something like:

- "I can't help you unless you let me."
- "We're in this together."
- "What part of this *can* you agree to?"
- "I can see that this has really upset you. Although our sales quotas are important, thinking outside the box, what might you be able to do to reach the minimum?"

Your goal during performance coaching conversations is to have the PBC own the situation. Your role is to share the purpose with the PBC and then allow the PBC to determine how he or she will fix the issue or close the gap.

If PBCs do not agree that there is an issue, problem, or gap, your role is not to force it on them, but possibly to figure out the underlying reason for this resistance. Are they afraid to admit they don't know something because they don't want to show a weakness, do they not like to be challenged or told that they don't know something or are not performing to standard, or are they truly unaware of the gap? Many times your role as the coach will be to help PBCs know what they don't know or see what they don't see.

Coaches do not confront others about their performance to make them angry, upset, defensive, or depressed. They do so in order to change performance. They do not set out to stimulate negative emotions in others. But, in spite of how disciplined and skilled you are in addressing performance issues, some level of negative emotion can still be generated. Knowing how to use the negative reactions of others to gain agreement is helpful when coaching.

Focus on the Future

To help reduce resistance, once you have clarified the purpose, let the PBC determine *what* needs to happen to fix the issue and *how* they will go about it. Stay focused on the future; it is much less threatening for a person to talk about what can be fixed (the future) than it is for a person to talk about what cannot be fixed (the past). This does not mean that the past is not important and that a discussion of causes for a problem should not occur. It means only that the coach must create an environment for the conversation that implicitly says, "I want to focus on what can be changed, such as performance, not blame you for what is wrong" or "I want you to know something," not "I think you're an idiot for not knowing this already."

In the case of performance problems, some people indicate explicit ownership of a problem by saying something like, "I recognize that I should have checked these priorities out with you before I assumed which ones were most important." Others may indicate implicit ownership by describing what they are going to do to fix a problem, but never admit ownership of the problem, for example, "I'll turn in the budget to you by the end of the day." It is not always important that people explicitly state that they are responsible for a problem. What is important is that they state how they are going to fix the problem.

A fundamental principle of continuous improvement is to make it as easy as possible for people to improve. It is often easier for people to accept responsibility for fixing performance problems than it is for them to admit that they have made a mistake or failed in some way. As a coach, it is best to recognize that *ownership has occurred when people give a clear and sincere signal that they are going to fix the performance problem or improve proficiency—even if they never explicitly say that they are responsible for the problem in the first place.* In other words, don't make them grovel if they are willing to fix it. Being willing, in this case, equals acknowledgement and agreement, and agreement is far more powerful than humiliation.

In summary, allow the PBC to talk, vent, explore, solve the issue, and create an action plan, even when you were the one communicating the *why* and your expectations. Be careful not to ask leading questions to guide the PBC to your ideas, solutions, or hidden agendas. Don't move forward too quickly if emotions or resistance are still high. Move forward when the PBC is willing to accept ownership and offer a course of action that moves him or her forward toward correcting the performance issue. Your advanced planning will help this go smoothly, even if you don't do everything exactly as planned.

To assist you with planning for your performance coaching conversation or any conversation in which you bring the *why* to the table, use the Performance Coaching Worksheet in Exhibit 7.1. The first section is all about the components that should be included in your opening dialog; the second set of questions are to further prepare you for more difficult conversations. Planning for these sessions may take a little more time at first, but after a while, will become more natural and progress more quickly.

Exhibit 7.1. Performance Coaching Worksheet

PBC: **Coach:**   **Date:**

Use this form to prepare for your performance coaching conversations, when you bring the *why* (*Why* are we having this conversation?) to the person being coached (PBC).

COACH'S OPENING . . .

Why is this conversation necessary? (Be specific.) How will I introduce it?

What does the PBC need to know about the situation and my expectations? (Most recent behavior versus expectations.)

What is the impact of the PBC's behavior on him or her, on me, the team, and/or the company?

How will I shift ownership so that the PBC owns the problem, gap, or issue? What question can I start with?

BEING FULLY PREPARED . . .

When and where will the coaching take place?

How will I eliminate distractions?

What will I say to establish and maintain trust?

How will I set the PBC at ease?

What is my ideal outcome? (If not ideal, what is the best I could hope for?)

How will I react if the PBC doesn't agree with my assessment?

If necessary, how will I depersonalize the situation?

What can I say to reduce resistance and/or remain focused on the future?

Are there things I need to own up to? (Was I unclear? Is there an unusually heavy workload?) How can I communicate those things?

What positive feedback or acknowledgements will I use?

What is my timeline for visible progress?

What are my follow-up needs/commitments from the PBC?

What documents or data must be gathered before the meeting?

Additional Comments:

Documentation

If you are going to use facts, numbers, reports, policies, or procedures in your coaching conversations or if you suspect that you may need to produce proof for the PBC, have the necessary documentation handy before the coaching session.

Following are some tips for gathering documentation:

- Have facts at the ready that you can point to in difficult moments.

- The same is true for data and numbers (spreadsheets, service levels, reports, etc.)

- Have key documents (or copies) close by and handy so that when they are needed, searching for them doesn't distract from the conversation.

- Compliance policies/regulations should be within reach so that you can provide clarity when needed.

- If this is a training or development conversation, have the applicable training material or policies close by for referral.

If you take notes during your coaching conversations, have previously taken notes readily available for reference.

Note-Taking

It is common for coaches to take notes during coaching conversations, but not a requirement. Note-taking is a personal preference and is a widely accepted practice by both the coach and PBC.

If you plan to take notes, prepare the PBC by letting him or her know your intention and try not to take so many notes that you are distracted or stop listening. Note-taking should be for the purpose of enhancing the coaching conversation and not a distraction. You can mention to the PBC that he or she is welcome to take notes as well.

If you do take notes, sometimes it is helpful to review the previous coaching session notes before you meet with your PBC again. This will refresh your memory of the action items you want to follow up on and allow you to refer back to previous commitments. It also allows you to follow up by using the PBC's language from the previous session.

- "Megan, how are you doing at going from feeling 'restricted' to 'liberated'?
- "Rob, how is your new motto of 'not sweating the small stuff' working for you?"

If you are note-taker, be sure to honor confidentiality by adequately securing your notes and/or using encrypted names/initials or some type of shorthand on the documents. If someone gets hold of your notes, would you be concerned about what you have written?

Use the Coach Notes, Exhibit 7.2, for your note-taking needs.

Coaching Channels

As mentioned, there are a variety of means, or coaching channels, by which successful coaching conversations are conducted. Coaching has historically occurred through face-to-face interaction, but with the advent of new technology, this has evolved to include virtual means of coaching, including phone, teleconference, email, videoconference, or web conference.

Although virtual coaching has encountered some resistance and controversy, *all* of the methods of coaching listed above can be *equally* effective. In fact, a coach can obtain far-reaching and phenomenal results from the PBC using any of these methods.

Corporate America, in many ways, is still getting comfortable with the notion of doing business by remote means. Thus, many internal company coaches (and human resources colleagues) are still more comfortable with face-to-face coaching. In addition, some consultants who are accustomed to doing their work face-to-face with their clients may be more inclined to gravitate toward face-to-face coaching, which we suggest may stem more from the coach's needs than the PBC's. Because we have evolved into a global society, it is important to embrace the technology that is offered to us. Go virtual!

Exhibit 7.2. Coach's Notes

Use this as your guide for conducting your coaching conversations and capturing notes.

Name (PBC):   Coach: Date:

Shift to Coach Role!				

InDiCom Coaching Model

INVOLVE

Purpose and Expectations
PBC accepted ownership
Identified gap

DISCOVER

Root causes (core issues)
PBC's ideas and solutions

COMMIT

PBC's plan of action
Roadblocks/obstacles discussed
PBC's recap
Follow-up plans

CLEAR

CHALLENGE	LISTEN	ENCOURAGE	ASK	REFINE
Request	Story Telling	Validate	Coaching Questions	Two-Words
Reality Check	Benefits of Silence	Celebrate	Powerful Statements	Metaphors

Notes for Next Meeting

Remember to ask about during the next session:

Key areas PBC is working on:

The reality is that virtual coaching is here! There is much coaching being conducted virtually these days within companies, between remote teams and teammates, as well as between external coaches and their corporate/private clients. It is effective, cost-effective, and time-efficient, and it serves a need to deliver real-time coaching as well as just-in-time coaching in a fast-paced, ever-changing environment. As a coach, have an open mind and try it if you haven't done so already.

Chapter 6, CLEAR Coaching Skills, explained that *all* of the skills could be applied to the virtual coaching conversation as much as the face-to-face session. Of course, you as coach will need to be much more astute in your Listen skill when conducting a phone coaching session and certainly more honed in your Ask skill when working by phone and by email. Virtual coaches are often *more skilled* out of necessity. You must have the ability to hear what is not being said, use your intuition, listen for ill-timed pauses from a PBC, recognize hesitation, emotions, and feelings through tone, etc. Virtual coaches are diligent in following the InDiCom coaching model. One other thing that virtual coaches must learn to do well is to eliminate distractions; multitasking is absolutely forbidden! Many of these things can easily be taken for granted in the face-to-face coaching conversation.

If thus far you have been a proponent of predominantly face-to-face coaching, ask yourself this: Can a blind person make a good coach? Of course he or she could! When a person loses the use of one sense, such as sight, other senses—intuition, hearing, smell, touch—all become naturally much more acute, in tune, and refined. Thus, the other senses recognize what the eyes cannot. The same is true of virtual coaches. As you coach virtually, you will find that your other senses compensate for what your eyes cannot see. If you are still a skeptic, next time you are on the phone with someone, try blindfolding yourself or closing your eyes during the conversation and concentrate on how much more acute your sense of hearing becomes and how much more aware you are of silences or pauses and tone. You may be surprised by what you experience and learn. You will also find that relying on your intuition becomes much more important.

Coaching Tools

Coaches use two common tools to enhance coaching effectiveness, especially when working with people managers and leaders—job shadowing and 360-degree feedback.

Job shadowing is where the coach follows and observes the PBC for a designated period of time or during a specific event, for example, conducting a meeting or presentation. Job shadowing is used by some coaches to gather insight into the PBC's actions and behaviors. It can have a place in some coaching situations and would most often require face-to-face interaction, although job shadowing alone *is not* coaching. Feedback given after a shadowing session is not the same as coaching unless it is delivered using a coaching model (such as InDiCom) and skills (like CLEAR) as a performance coaching conversation, where the PBC owns the *what* and *how*.

The downside of using job shadowing as a coaching tool is that when PBCs know they are being shadowed, they may have a tendency to step "on stage" and perform differently than usual. Intentionally or unintentionally, the PBC can act out, act up, or act differently than normal, which leaves the coach without a true sense or feel of what is happening.

It is also unlikely that the people around the PBC will feel comfortable being a party to apparent job-shadowing situations and may change their behavior accordingly. Although job shadowing may have its place in certain coaching situations, it is better suited for use in the *manager* or *mentor* roles. Job shadowing may give you a snapshot of what's happening, but it's not likely to give you the full picture and thus it is not the most effective way for determining coaching gaps.

What do you use instead? You can obtain significantly more information and insight into the PBC's actions and behaviors by anonymous 360-degree feedback gathering through assessments and/or anonymous interviews with key stakeholders. This helps to identify patterns of behavior, career derailers, and other necessary coaching gaps. There are many types of 360-degree assessments available, and most measure performance against a defined set of competencies. (The CSI:Observer can be used for evaluating coaching performance and skill.)

360-degree assessments collect the opinions of the PBC as well as those of peers, direct reports, partners, the boss, and other stakeholders as identified by the PBC. Because the feedback process is almost always anonymous, it has a greater tendency to be truthful, direct, and accurate. This information allows both coach and PBC to see overarching themes regarding the PBC's behavior. Equipped with this detailed information, PBCs can measure their perception of themselves against those of others, then choose how to use that data to identify and close relevant coaching gaps. Even if a PBC does not agree with the feedback or knows who it came from, ask him or her to assume that all of the feedback data is true so that he or she recognizes what perceptions are there and can then choose how to address them. PBCs can choose whether or not to change behaviors and/or they can figure out how to manage perceptions around patterns of behaviors that they didn't realize were evident or being portrayed.

The gap that needs to be addressed is often the misunderstanding between perceptions. This becomes the coaching goal, and subsequently action plans are developed by the PBC, to close the gap and make positive changes. In rare cases, if a PBC chooses to do nothing about the feedback received, because coaching is all about the PBC, this is his or her prerogative. When this happens, help PBCs explore the consequences and impacts of this inaction.

Coaching Moment

Current Reality: How do you currently conduct your performance coaching conversations? What channel of coaching are you most comfortable with?

Ideal State: What positive outcomes would be achieved by applying the tools and concepts in this chapter? What coaching channel would you like to try or become more comfortable with?

Action Plan: If you were to implement one or more of the ideas and tools from this chapter, what would you do differently from what you are doing now?

Chapter Summary

Performance Coaching

Performance coaching conversations can provide challenges in gaining ownership and encountering resistance from PBCs. Proper planning using the Performance Coaching Worksheet can provide a means for success. (See the sample performance coaching conversations in Chapter 8.)

Note-Taking

Note-taking is a personal preference. Notes are useful for enhancing coaching conversations as they are occurring, as well as a quick refresher for future ones. Respect privacy and confidentiality by encrypting and/or securing your notes.

Preparing for a performance coaching conversation is not the same as taking notes during your coaching sessions. Use the Performance Coaching Worksheet to *prepare* when you bring the *why* to the PBC. Use the Coach Notes Worksheet to capture notes *during* your coaching sessions.

Coaching Channels

There are several methods to conduct coaching conversations, all of which are equally effective:

- Face-to-Face (in person)
- Virtual—phone or conference call, email, videoconference, or web conference

Coaching Tools

360-degree feedback assessments are powerful tools for gathering anonymous insight into PBCs' actions and behaviors from multiple sources and based on certain competences. 360-degree feedback tools are an effective alternative to job shadowing.

CHAPTER 8

The Complete Coaching Conversation

"We come to beginnings only at the end."

—William Bridges

THIS CHAPTER CONTAINS complete coaching conversation examples, two coaching moment examples, and an email coaching example. Each of these samples combines the use of the InDiCom coaching model and the CLEAR coaching skills. Each also assumes a trust relationship has been established between the coach and the person being coached (PBC).

The length, setting, purpose, and players in each of these conversations vary. When reading through the examples, try to set aside any biases and keep in mind your collective learning. Also note that almost all of these conversations could have been conducted using any coaching channel (face-to-face or virtual).

It is a good idea to have a copy of the model and skills handy while you read through this section in order to identify the specific skills and stages that occur throughout the coaching conversations presented.

General Coaching—PBC's Why
Coaching Conversation

In this scenario, the coach could be the PBC's manager, peer, or partner. JJ, the PBC, is looking for guidance from Michelle (coach) on what appears to be a work/life balance issue. JJ is introducing the *why* to the conversation.

PBC/JJ: "Hi, Michelle, I've been meaning to ask you about something that's really been bothering me lately."

COACH/MICHELLE: "I'd love to help. What's going on?"

PBC/JJ: "How do people balance work life and home life?"

COACH/MICHELLE: "That's the hottest question of the decade! Why don't you tell me more about what you're struggling with."

PBC/JJ: "I work late every day and never feel caught up or that I'll ever have the chance to catch up. I could work 24/7 and never get caught up."

COACH/MICHELLE: "Wow! That must feel like an awful burden to go home with every night. What seems to be the biggest demand on your time?"

PBC/JJ: "I love my employees and I know they love me. They come to me for everything and I love knowing that I've helped them."

COACH/MICHELLE: "Tell me more about how your interaction with your employees ties into your never feeling caught up."

PBC/JJ: "I spend so much time 'coaching' other people every day; I don't have time to get to the projects that I've committed to."

COACH/MICHELLE: "JJ, let's explore why your employees are coming to you for so many things. What do they need from you?"

PBC/JJ: "They need answers and I have them. They need to know how to do their jobs. They need to know how to respond to customers. The list goes on."

COACH/MICHELLE: "What should they be coming to you for?"

PBC/JJ: "Hmmm, good question, Michelle. I thought they should be coming to me for everything I just mentioned, but maybe not."

COACH/MICHELLE: "Really, tell me more, JJ."

PBC/JJ: "I'm supposed to be their leader, but I can see that all I've really taught them is to come to me for everything, and I will do it for them. But, based on what we learned in the Coaching for Commitment workshop last week, that isn't really coaching, is it?"

COACH/MICHELLE: "It's great that you can see that telling and solving is not coaching, because it doesn't help them get their own answers, and it certainly doesn't help you to work any fewer hours! You are off to a great start here. So JJ, now what do you see as the real issue?"

PBC/JJ: "That I've taught them to be dependent on me for everything."

COACH/MICHELLE: "People treat you how you teach them to treat you. If you could create your ideal, what would that look like?"

PBC/JJ: "People coming to me for strategic decisions or leadership ideas, and maybe to identify other resources, but not to solve every little issue, or answer every question they have."

COACH/MICHELLE: "So, if you could describe where things are currently using one word, what would that one word be?"

PBC/JJ: "Caretaker."

COACH/MICHELLE: "What would you want that one word to be?"

PBC/JJ: "Coach."

COACH/MICHELLE: "What will it take for you to move from being a caretaker to a coach?"

PBC/JJ: "I have to let them solve things on their own and not make them so dependent on me."

COACH/MICHELLE: "I'd like for you to think about something. Are they coming to you now because they really need your knowledge, or have you taught them to need your approval before they can move forward?"

PBC/JJ: "Hmmm, it's not the first one, and I don't have to approve everything they do. . . . I guess if I am really honest with myself, it is that I've needed them to come to me so I know what they're doing. I guess that is because I want to be prepared if something goes wrong or so I can deal with any fallout of their actions—if it comes to that."

COACH/MICHELLE: "So they really don't need you to solve these things for them? You just need the information so you feel comfortable."

PBC/JJ: "Yes, I think so."

COACH/MICHELLE: "What can you do to start making a shift in how you behave?"

PBC/JJ: "When they come to me I can ask them what they're going to do first and let them know their idea was great. Soon they won't need to come to me for 'perceived' answers they already know."

COACH/MICHELLE: "That is a very workable idea. What else can you do, JJ?"

PBC/JJ: "I can talk with them. Let them know they don't need to check in with me all of the time if they know what to do. I have to let them know I trust them."

COACH/MICHELLE: "Yes! Letting them know you trust them is a great idea."

PBC/JJ: "I guess I thought they would already know that."

COACH/MICHELLE: "What specifically will you do to display trust and be more of a 'coach' and not their 'caretaker'?"

PBC/JJ: "I need to do what you're doing right now, ask more questions. I need to let people come up with their own solutions and let them try their solutions."

COACH/MICHELLE: "What is the worst thing that could happen if you do this?"

PBC/JJ: "They may make mistakes!"

COACH/MICHELLE: "And what would be the consequences of their mistakes?"

PBC/JJ: "It depends on the mistake! Some would be worse than others."

COACH/MICHELLE: "And . . . ?"

PBC/JJ: "I guess I didn't want them to make any mistakes."

COACH/MICHELLE: "What are you afraid of?"

PBC/JJ: "Failure. And that I would look bad."

COACH/MICHELLE: "Fear leads to control. Where can you give up some control so you're not afraid to fail?"

PBC/JJ: "I need to let them make mistakes in the area of decisions that are not critical."

COACH/MICHELLE: "Does this sound like something you're willing to try?"

PBC/JJ: "Yes, it feels good! Kind of liberating. I don't like that I am always so worried about everything. If I can share the worry, maybe it won't seem so overwhelming and then I can make the most of my home time."

COACH/MICHELLE: "Good segue, JJ. Coming back to the original reason you came to me, in what other ways will this help you with your work and home-life balance?"

PBC/JJ: "If I'm not doing everybody else's work, I would probably have time throughout the day for my own. Then maybe I can go home on time!"

COACH/MICHELLE: "What do you think will be your biggest obstacle?"

PBC/JJ: "Myself! This will be a big change for me and I can see myself falling back into solving their problems for them. I have to realize that giving them my solution is not always better, even though it seems faster and less risky. I also have to remember that it might take a few more minutes up-front, but it will get me to where I want to be in the end. Plus, I got where I am by making mistakes and because people gave me the opportunity to learn from them. I have to let my team have the same chances to do that. I have to get out of the way for us all to be more successful."

COACH/MICHELLE: "What are a couple of ways you can think of to remind yourself of these things when they occur?"

PBC/JJ: "Well, I could start by letting my employees know that I'm going to be making some changes in my approach and why. Then they can help me be accountable to myself and them. Next, when they come to me I can deliberately pause before I make a response to one of their questions to ask myself if they really need the answer from me. Then, I can ask them questions about their comfort level with dealing with each situation and make decisions on a case by case basis about how much autonomy can be given and what the risks are. Oh, better yet, I can get them to problem solve and do a risk assessment as a part of the conversation and their own learning! I think I am catching on!"

COACH/MICHELLE: "Those all sound like very effective actions, JJ. I think you'll be surprised by how quickly you can begin to have more successful coaching conversations just by implementing these ideas. You did well at figuring this out and making some commitments to achieve your goal! How do you feel about your newfound freedom?"

PBC/JJ: "I can't wait to go back and get started with the new me!"

COACH/MICHELLE: "Before you go, can you please tell me in a few sentences what you are taking away from our conversation?"

PBC/JJ: "That I'm the one responsible for not having any time at the end of the day because I've made my people dependent on me for answers. I don't need to solve everything for them and, if I trust them, I'll have more time for being their leader. That I need to think about how much I trust them and how/where it's okay for them to make mistakes so they can learn."

COACH/MICHELLE: "I think you had some real eye-openers today, and I'm really impressed with your willingness to try something so new for you. I'd like to hear how it goes. This will be an ongoing process that I'd like to help you transition through. When would you like to follow up and share how things are going?"

PBC/JJ: "Thanks, Michelle, this was really helpful! I don't want to shock my employees, but I'm ready to try some new things right away and I think that they are more than ready for me to get out of the way. I think I should have something to report back to you as early as next week. How about if I call you on Thursday at 1?"

COACH/MICHELLE: "Thursday works for me. I look forward to hearing all about your success!"

Take a moment to think about this coaching session. What stood out to you? What pieces did you like? Were there parts that you would not have been comfortable with? If so, how would you have handled or said things differently and yet achieved the same result? (Remember, you're not giving advice in the *coach role*.)

Keeping the InDiCom coaching model in mind, when did the conversation transition from one stage of the model to the next? Did it ever move backward in the stages and then forward again? What CLEAR coaching skills were used?

You may also note that, even though the *why* belongs to JJ, that this is a conversation that could easily be had if Michelle had started the conversation to address JJ's lack of balance or even micro-management. During the course of your coaching conversations, no matter who identifies the *why*, you never know when a core issue will come up (such as fear of failure, lack of work/life balance, not trusting employees or giving them enough independence, etc.). Be ready to go there when it happens.

Coaching Conversation 2

In this scenario, the coach (Rachael) is a peer and the PBC (Jason) is asking for some help on an upcoming presentation (the *why*). Note how easily Rachael slips into the *coach role*. Also notice how natural the flow of the conversation is, even though she doesn't tell Jason that she's coaching him. Although we are certainly advocates for sharing the language of coaching with others, this example illustrates that, even if the PBC doesn't know what coaching is, it can still be effective.

PBC/JASON: "Rachael, I need your help. I've been asked to give a presentation next week and I'm scared to death. I hate speaking in front of people; it makes me a nervous wreck. I've seen you present before and you make it look so easy. Can you help me? This presentation is really important for me."

COACH/RACHAEL: "I'd be delighted to help you, Jason. Tell me a little bit more about what you've been asked to do."

PBC/JASON: "Well, they gave me twenty minutes to show them a new product our team would like to put into production. Someone on our team had a great idea, and in order for us to be able to spend any time and money on it, we need to get this group of managers to give us the okay."

COACH/RACHAEL: "Great. So the managers are your target audience?"

PBC/JASON: "Yeah, ten of them who intimidate the heck out of me."

COACH/RACHAEL: "Don't worry, Jason! We'll make sure you're ready and that you take away their power to intimidate you. I've seen you do presentations to other groups; I know you can do it!"

PBC/JASON: "I hope so. I am just so nervous and don't feel prepared at all!"

COACH/RACHAEL: "Alright, so which would you like to focus on? Nerves or preparedness?"

PBC/JASON: "I think if I felt more prepared, I could overcome the nerves."

COACH/RACHAEL: "Let's start there then. Let me see if I have things straight so we can focus better. You are scheduled to do a presentation of a new product idea to ten senior managers. And it sounds like you need their approval to move forward with producing the product your team thought up. Do I have that right?"

PBC/JASON: "That's about it."

COACH/RACHAEL: "First of all, congratulations on coming up with a new product you think will benefit the company and for being willing to present it. Now, I need to find out a few more things."

PBC/JASON: "Okay, what do you need to know?"

COACH/RACHAEL: "You need their buy-in and their signoff. What role does your manager play in this?"

PBC/JASON: "My manager is in full support of it. She's the one who asked me to present it to the management team because she wants me to share my team's great idea. She'll be at the meeting. She said she'll stand behind me and support me."

COACH/RACHAEL: "Great, Jason. Having someone in there you know is on your side should make things easier for you. Does she know what role you want her to play in your presentation?"

PBC/JASON: "Well, she's really excited for me. I guess I need to ask her to be supportive in her comments and be our cheerleader when the others throw up roadblocks. I think she would do that."

COACH/RACHAEL: "That sounds great. Now let's get into what you need to do to prepare for this presentation. Think about the managers you will be presenting to. What do you want these managers to know about your team's idea?"

PBC/JASON: "I want them to know how the new product will be a great hit with our customers. I know our customers need it; they ask for it all the time, and we always have to tell them we don't have anything like it."

COACH/RACHAEL: "So you want them to know how this will benefit the customer and how it will fill a need that the customers have been asking for?"

PBC/JASON: "Yep."

COACH/RACHAEL: "If someone were to come to you trying to sell you something, what types of questions would *you* need answered?"

PBC/JASON: "I would want to know the who, where, what, how, and why for starters."

COACH/RACHAEL: "Good. What if you were skeptical? What would you need to hear then?"

PBC/JASON: "I would need to know more about what the benefits of this product are and maybe how it serves to cut costs or at least not increase them. I would also want to make sure that the planning phase and the production phase move smoothly so that there is no lag time that costs the company extra money. So I guess that means I'd want to know that the product manager has done his homework and has thought through the possible problems in advance."

COACH/RACHAEL: "Yes! And how could you present that information in a way that gets the managers as excited as you and your team are?"

PBC/JASON: "Well, let's see, I would have to have a polished presentation so that I won't be nervous and I'd need to let my natural excitement shine through, I guess. And the presentation would have to include the components I just mentioned, maybe a tentative product plan and some numbers to show we have done the due diligence. I would also want some of my team there to chime in—I think that would help! Hey, I'm getting excited about this already. You've given me a lot to think about, but I do have one other question. Tell me, exactly *how* should I present this?"

COACH/RACHAEL: "What do you think would be best?"

PBC/JASON: "Hmmmm ... for starters, I think it would be good to show them our prototype—do an unveiling with a red drape and then some drama. But there also has to be substance. . . ."

COACH/RACHAEL: "Keep going, this is sounding exciting!"

PBC/JASON: "I should have a PowerPoint deck and maybe I could get one of my team to share the stage with me. I wouldn't be so nervous that way and he or she could talk through the technicalities while I handle the numbers and planning pieces. I would love to find a way to make this interactive to some extent so the managers really sink their teeth into it. Maybe I could leave them with something ... too bad we can't make mini prototypes by next week, but I think I'll take that one back to the team and we can brainstorm it."

COACH/RACHAEL: "This is great stuff, Jason!"

PBC/JASON: "Yeah, I think it could work and I am feeling more confident already. Have I missed anything?"

COACH/RACHAEL: "I think you have your bases covered, but let's explore obstacles just in case. Any you can think of?"

PBC/JASON: "Only the ones the managers may throw up!"

COACH/RACHAEL: "How can you plan for those?"

PBC/JASON: "My team and I will prepare a list of possible responses for the devil's advocate types. We have already looked at all the pros and cons, so it is just a matter of having a formal answer at the ready."

COACH/RACHAEL: "Wow! You really are ahead of the game! How are you feeling about this presentation now?"

PBC/JASON: "I am psyched!"

COACH/RACHAEL: "What further support can I provide you?"

PBC/JASON: "You've done a lot already, Rachael, but I would like to have you look at what we put together. Why don't I work on it, meet with my team, gel the strategy a little, and then I would love to present to you before the meeting next week and get your feedback. Would that be okay?"

COACH/RACHAEL: "I can't wait to see what you come up with; even I am excited!"

PBC/JASON: "Thanks, Rachael, I knew you were the right one to come to."

COACH/RACHAEL: "You're welcome, Jason. I want you to be successful with your presentation, too. Let me know if you need help before your dry run or if I can answer any other questions."

PBC/JASON: "I will! Have a great day!"

In what ways did Jason take accountability for his part? Can you identify the skills Rachael used and where the steps of the model transitioned?

Performance Coaching—Coach's Why

In the next two coaching scenarios, the coach brings the (*why* all we having this conversation?) to the table in order to address gaps in performance with each PBC.

Coaching Conversation 3

In this scenario, the coach is the PBC's manager, Gwen. Even though Gwen is the PBC's (Martha's) boss, right now she is in the *coach role* and is addressing a gap in Martha's performance. Gwen is bringing the *why* to the table in this conversation.

COACH/GWEN: "Hi, Martha. I asked you to come in today because I am concerned about you and your team. I've noticed that you have been struggling in getting the accounts payable reports to me on time for at least two weeks now. You have never missed deadlines before, and I'd like to know what's happening."

PBC/MARTHA: "Ugh! I know! And I knew you were eventually going to ask me about this, Gwen. I just don't know where to start. . . . I know we are falling behind and it just keeps getting worse! I am trying to find time to figure out the ins and outs and shortcuts of this new cash register system, but we have been so slammed lately, I can't put my workload aside long enough to spend any extra time on it. We are all struggling with this thing. The way it's set up now, we have more manual work that needs to be done to create the accounts payable reports than we did before. And no one bothered to ask us what we needed in terms of a new system, so now we are backlogged because it doesn't really do what we need it to do. It just does what some techie thought it should, and the best we can do are work-arounds. These take much longer, which is why the reports have been late."

COACH/GWEN: "Wow. I can tell you are really frustrated about this. It is a tough situation to be in. I know the new system and a heavy workload really have you and your team hopping, and I wish you had come to me about your concerns. I'm also glad you are here now. Martha, how would you feel about letting me coach you through this situation?"

PBC/MARTHA: "That would be great! I could use some coaching on this one. I seem to be stuck at figuring out a solution, and I'm sorry I didn't come to you sooner. I thought we'd have it under control by now."

COACH/GWEN: "Why don't you restate for me what you see as the core issue."

PBC/MARTHA: "Sure. I don't have any extra time to learn the new cash register system in-depth, and my team and I are getting further behind in our work."

COACH/GWEN: "It sounds like the new system is a big part of the issue. Tell me more."

PBC/MARTHA: "We all went through the two-hour introductory training and that was fine, but when it came time to actually use this system and generate reports from the data, it just wasn't there!"

COACH/GWEN: "Martha, what exactly do you mean by, 'It just wasn't there'?"

PBC/MARTHA: "Exactly that. A portion of the data that we needed to create the accounts payable report is something that appears to have to be input manually because the new cash register system doesn't capture that data nor separate it out like the old system did. So in order to give you your report, we have to manually sort through the data, and that takes time that we don't have because we are still learning the new system and because we now have that extra work to do on top of the standard demands for handling payroll refunds and payments, which also use the new system. Not to mention our skeleton staffing situation."

COACH/GWEN: "Martha, you keep mentioning the time versus task issue, and I can see that that is a part of the problem. Are there any other major issues that you can separate out?"

PBC/MARTHA: "The system doesn't do what we need it to do."

COACH/GWEN: "Yes, it seems that is the case. Can you share with me what exactly you need it to do?"

PBC/MARTHA: "Yes. It needs to be able to separate out specific pieces of the input data so that we can pull a query that feeds your report. Or it needs to provide subtotals of categories so that we can more easily pull the numbers we need to compile a separate report for you, if the system can't do it. Of course, it would be better if it captured the data and sorted it like the old system, but I think we've given up on that."

COACH/GWEN: "And what would your recommendations be for making one of these things happen?"

PBC/MARTHA: "There are a couple of possibilities. One, if the data is there the way we need it, and I am pretty sure it isn't, we need to know that once and for all. Second, if the subtotal alternative is possible, we need to know that as well. The only way for us to find that out is to know the system inside and out, and we don't. So we need either time to learn it or more training on it. Finally, if the data is not there and not available, then we either need to find another system, which I am guessing is not an option since we just got this one and that about killed this year's budget, or we look at bringing on an additional resource dedicated to reporting so that they can work the reporting piece while we handle the rest."

COACH/GWEN: "These are all good ideas. Tell me, which of these ideas seems the most workable to you?"

PBC/MARTHA: "It depends on whether we can find out if the system has what we need."

COACH/GWEN: "Are there any other ways you can think of for going about that?"

PBC/MARTHA: "So far, I've tried everything I can think of, and Bill spent hours last week searching the training material and online help for the right answers."

COACH/GWEN: "Any other ideas?"

PBC/MARTHA: "I guess we could call the company and get the rep on the phone who sold it to us. Since we weren't involved in the decision, I didn't think we could go that route."

COACH/GWEN: "You are right, Martha. You should have been included in the decision to buy the new software. Since you weren't, I think your idea to contact the company is a great one. This could help you figure out a lot! How can you make that happen?"

PBC/MARTHA: "I'll call Bettina as soon as we are done here and find out who the rep was and then make the call. That may really be the help we are looking for."

COACH/GWEN: "Do you foresee any challenges in following through with this?"

PBC/MARTHA: "Not really, Gwen. Just if we don't get the answer we are hoping for."

COACH/GWEN: "I hope you do. And if you don't, your other idea of obtaining a resource for the reporting is not out of the question. We have been talking about getting your team some help for a while now. This may be the catalyst to do so. We can always hire some temporary help for you until you get this sorted out. In fact, you can do that today if you need to. The budget may be tight, but I think we can make a solid business case."

PBC/MARTHA: "Really? Oh, that would be wonderful! We are really dying out there right now. Even without the cash register issue, there is more work coming in than ever. The team will be thrilled to hear this!"

COACH/GWEN: "And I'll be thrilled to get my reports on time again! Martha, what is the first thing you are going to do when you leave my office today?"

PBC/MARTHA: "I am going to find out the number for the sales and support rep for that darn cash register system and get on the horn!"

COACH/GWEN: "Good for you! How will I know how it goes and what you need from me?"

PBC/MARTHA: "Do you have time tomorrow afternoon at around 4 p.m.? I should know something by then."

COACH/GWEN: "Tomorrow at 4 it is then. Thanks for coming in, Martha, and good luck!"

How did Gwen use the CLEAR coaching skills to make this an effective interaction? How did Gwen maintain trust between herself and Martha? When did Martha take ownership of the problem? How did Gwen's use of the CLEAR skills encourage Martha to take ownership?

Coaching Conversation 4

This conversation is a twist on the typical performance coaching conversation. Heidi, the coach, is the PBC's (Lynn's) manager and she needs some additional help training the hospital employees on a new system. Heidi knows Lynn is going to resist because she hates systems training. This conversation isn't about a gap in performance; it's about a gap in confidence and a request that will stretch both Lynn's time and comfort level. Note how well Heidi stays in the *coach role*.

COACH/HEIDI: "Lynn, I asked you to come in to talk to me because I am in a position where I need your help covering training for a while. With two of your co-workers out on maternity leave, I am about to ask you to do something that I know you don't want to do, and something I know you have been avoiding."

PBC/LYNN: "Oh no, Heidi, please don't tell me I have to train that awful new PARC system! That thing is always being upgraded! You know how technology challenged I am, and what about my other classes? There is no way I can continue to cover my current classes and do this, too!"

COACH/HEIDI: "I don't like this any better than you do, Lynn. I had hoped not to put you in this position, but my hands are tied. I really need you to step up to the plate on this one to help the team, me, and the hospital. This new revision of PARC is going to be a bear! One thing I do know is that, even if you don't like technology, when you do put your mind to learning something, like a new system, you know it better than anyone, and that is what I really need right now. Is there a way we can both get what we want here?"

PBC/LYNN: "Well, what I really want is for the PARC system to go away, but if it did, I'm sure something else would take its place and then I'd still have to train it! I know you are in a bind and I want to be a team player. If there is any way that I can keep some of my existing classes—you know, the ones I *like* to train—in order to break this up a bit, then sure, I can help."

COACH/HEIDI: "First, I appreciate your willingness to help me out and it really will help the team meet their goals for the year, so thank you for that! Second, yes, you can keep some of your existing classes and I can make sure that training the new system is a shared responsibility for the remainder of the team. Because this all hinges on you, I want your input on everything from soup to nuts. Let's start with what your ideas on how to shift your workload so you can begin to learn the new system. I will need you to begin training at least two sessions a week on the new system by next month. How can you meet this goal?"

PBC/LYNN: "Well, I guess first I will need to brush up on that training manual that Ruth created at the start of this thing and then, well, I will need to shadow with someone who has been using it—that will take at least a week. Then, I think I will need some one-on-one time with Ruth, at least a few hours a day for a couple of days. In the meantime, I have to figure out a way to shift some of my current class load—at least half of it—to the remaining trainers we have left. I'm afraid you are going to have to take the heat on that one, boss! And my guess is that Ruth is also going to have to get some relief in her workload in order to help me out."

COACH/HEIDI: "No worries there, Lynn. I am already preparing for this week's team call where I will lay out the new training plan for the PARC system, including your involvement, and I will be asking for scheduling input into how we can cover the gaps. I think you have some good ideas. Where would you like to start?"

PBC/LYNN: "Why don't I talk with Hector first. He was the subject-matter expert on the training manual Ruth created. He also helped Sasha conduct the first few training classes. He could be a very valuable resource for me and may even let me shadow him. Hey, maybe he would be willing to train PARC *for* me!?" (laughs)

COACH/HEIDI: "I know you would do anything to get out of this one! Sorry, Lynn, it is still your job!" (laughs too)

PBC/LYNN: "It was worth a shot. Hey, when do I get to see the next set of enhancements on this thing?"

COACH/HEIDI: "I was told they were coming in from Kyle's software developers this afternoon."

PBC/LYNN: "Good, can I use your authority to get those?"

COACH/HEIDI: "Sure. How else can I help?"

PBC/LYNN: "Can you ask Nikki to cover my training this afternoon so I can start running down these fire drills?"

COACH/HEIDI: "I can and I would, but don't you think she might appreciate the word from you instead?"

PBC/LYNN: "Oh sure, make me the bad guy" (laughs). "I was just testin' ya, boss. I can ask her. I think she would be more than willing to cover for me if it's just an afternoon. And you'll be having the big training coverage talk at the team meeting tomorrow, so that should take care of things after that."

COACH/HEIDI: "I love your sense of humor, Lynn. Now, let's make sure we are on the same page. Can you tell me what your plan is going to be for the next couple of weeks?"

PBC/LYNN: "Sure. I am going to call Hector today and set up a meeting with him. Then, I am going to pull out Ruth's training manual, blow the dust off of it, and begin reading. I'll ask Nikki to cover at least my last class today so that I can do some studying and talk to Kyle about making those enhancements. In addition, I am going to talk to Ruth about working with me one-on-one, but only after I talk to Hector, to figure out the shadowing part."

COACH/HEIDI: "That sounds like a terrific plan, Lynn. I can't thank you enough for rising to this challenge. If for some reason Nikki can't cover your class today, please let me know. I can jump in for you if I need to. In fact, let me know whatever you need, I am here to support you. Speaking of which, when can you let me know about your progress?"

PBC/LYNN: "Hmmm. . . . Well, I guess I could check in with you every couple of days. You are usually here when I get here in the mornings, so we could chat then."

COACH/HEIDI: "That sounds like it will work for both of us. Thanks again, Lynn, I really do appreciate you, and happy learning!"

PBC/LYNN: "You're welcome, Heidi. See you later, and you owe me one!" (laughs)

As you can see, it was not necessary for Heidi to pummel Lynn in order to make progress. Coaching is not a battle of wills. A PBC can take ownership without having to grovel or set aside his or her needs. If you are clear in establishing the purpose and setting expectations in the Involve stage of the model, your PBC will more often than not be very receptive to coaching when you introduce the *why*. The other important thing to note in this conversation is that, even though the topic was serious, humor was still a natural part of the conversation!

Learning to move through this sequence can be difficult at first. It is human nature for us to feel responsible for addressing the issue and creating conflict as well as for fixing and solving. In *coach role*, you don't have to fix or solve for PBCs. They can do it on their own with you there as a coach to empower them. You can illuminate things (the *why*) so that PBCs have a chance to fix them, see them differently, find their own way, make their own shifts, and reach goals more effectively.

What else did you notice about this conversation?

Coaching Moments

Coaching moments can happen in two minutes or less. They are quick coaching conversations that reinforce, validate, celebrate, redirect, or revisit a previous coaching conversation topic. Most often, the coach brings the *why* to the coaching moment conversation. Occasionally it is the PBC. Think of a time when someone asked you a question that you could have turned into a coaching moment.

There are two coaching moment examples that follow. The first is a redirection of an employee by his boss. The second is a validation and celebration of improved performance based on a previous coaching conversation. In both, the coach brings the *why* to the conversation.

Coaching Conversation 5—Redirect

Doug was a new employee and was working as a stocker at a local home repair center. He was at the end of his aisle stocking shelves when a customer walked past with her hands full. The customer obviously picked up more items than expected and, with no cart, her large stack was being perilously balanced between her hands and chin. It wasn't long before the customer dropped an item from her load and was unable to pick it up from the floor without jeopardizing losing the rest of the items in her grip. Doug looked on, but didn't seem to register what was happening or realize that he could play a role in helping in this scenario, but another customer did. The passer-by picked up the dropped item and helped the customer arrange it once again under her chin. At that moment, Gina, Doug's manager (who was training him), came by and took in the scene. She waited until after the customer left and discreetly took Doug aside.

COACH/GINA: "Hi, Doug! I'm curious about your response to that customer just now. She was really struggling with her load and you didn't offer to help. Usually, you are very good about helping others. What happened?"

PBC/DOUG: "I would have helped her, but I didn't see any carts in the area to grab for her and I had to get the stocking finished before the end of my shift. I didn't want to leave any of the workload for someone else."

COACH/GINA: "Doug, I appreciate your sense of responsibility toward your job and, as your trainer and manager, feel I should clarify some things for you that I may have left unclear. Customers always come first in the store. If taking good care of our customers means that I need to jump in and help you with your duties or give you a few minutes of overtime to finish your work, that's okay! Now that you know this, how could you handle that situation with the customer differently next time?"

PBC/DOUG: "I would stop what I was doing and go get her a cart, make sure she was situated, and then I would go back to my stocking. Or I could have carried a few items for her to the checkout. And, if I couldn't get the stocking done, I would let you know and maybe even stay late to finish."

COACH/GINA: "I think you've got it! What are we in agree-ment on?"

PBC/DOUG: "Customers come first!"

COACH/GINA: "Terrific! See you later, Doug."

This is a perfect example of seeking first to understand. Doug, as a less experienced employee and maybe even a young person who doesn't have a lot of work or customer service experience, doesn't know what is expected of him at work and may not know how to ask. In addition, Gina didn't make any assumptions about why Doug didn't help the customer. She simply addressed what she saw and allowed him to explain, then come to his own conclusions. What else did Gina do that made this coaching moment successful?

Coaching Conversation 6—Celebrate

Junel, the coach, and Patsy, the PBC, recently had a coaching conversation during which a performance issue was addressed. Patsy, a teacher, wasn't doing a very good job of getting back to her classroom on time after lunch. Patsy was late seven days in one month, and her fellow teachers were starting to complain because the students were going unsupervised during that time. Junel, who is Patsy's department head, chose to use the *coach role* to address the problem. Two weeks later, Patsy has returned to her classroom on time every day after lunch, and some days she's been early—all part of Patsy's action plan after coaching. Junel has just observed Patsy returning early for the fifth day in a row. She is about to have a coaching moment to congratulate Patsy on a job well done.

COACH/JUNEL: "Patsy, do you have a minute?"

PBC/PATSY: "Sure, Junel, what's up?"

COACH/JUNEL: "I just wanted to let you know that I've noticed what an effort you have been making to get back from lunch on time and even early these days. I really appreciate your positive response and action to our coaching conversation two weeks ago."

PBC/PATSY: "Thanks, Junel, and thanks for noticing. I have really been working on it."

COACH/JUNEL: "I can tell, and so can others. Your fellow teachers have even commented. And this is the fifth day in a row you've been early!"

PBC/PATSY: "Well, that certainly makes it worth it! It's all about the team and kids as far as I'm concerned."

COACH/JUNEL: "It sure is. Keep up the great work, Patsy!"

PBC/PATSY: "Thanks, Junel. I will!"

What is the benefit of having a follow-up coaching moment such as this with a PBC?

Coaching by Email

Most often, email coaching is used in between coaching conversations for covering small, quick coaching topics or as a touch base between coach and PBC. In select cases, it can be used as the main coaching channel between a coach and a PBC. The following example is an illustration of the latter.

We live in a global society that offers us the means to maximize all of our communication options. Email coaching can be an effective, efficient, and cost-effective method for coaching.

Coaching Conversation 7

The following are excerpts, adapted from actual email coaching sessions, between an executive coach and a private client. The client, Minerva, was working with her coach, Floreen, for the purpose of changing career paths from her current career into another career path. Minerva, who was in the midst of an unfulfilling job in a toxic work environment, was looking to not only change jobs but potentially change vocations. This meant figuring out what her ideal job was and how to go about finding it in her small Midwestern town, or at least within a reasonable commute. Outside of this scope there would be further things to consider: relocation to a more thriving business community, family needs, personal needs, etc. Minerva was used to having her next job just fall into her lap. This is the first time that she would be calling all the shots and pursuing new opportunities on her own terms. As with any situation, there is always more to the picture. Life is complicated, and these kinds of decisions are not always cut and dry or simple! There is always more to coaching than what is on the surface.

Minerva is a devoted parent, wife, and family member with siblings who live in the same small town. She is bright, dynamic, and energetic and has goals that can take her to great heights. She has the experience to take her there as well. She is accustomed to always putting others' needs first, before her own, a habit she has been trying to break.

During a portion of her coaching, Minerva was a primary caregiver to a terminally ill parent. In addition, due to an existing custody agreement with her ex-spouse, there was a need to balance prudence with idealism in looking at jobs that required relocation. Because life is full of surprises, right around the time Minerva began her coaching sessions to find out what her ideal job should be, a job opportunity presented itself. At first, the role appeared to have all the makings of her ideal job. Everyone else, including Minerva's friends and spouse, thought so, too. This new opportunity came as the result of a harmless "informational visit" Minerva had made to a company she was researching. The company immediately started to aggressively pursue her for the position. Sounds great, right? Wrong! This put Minerva in the position to have to decide about not only a job change, but a career change, a quick relocation (despite her family concerns), and a position that turned out to have a lot of, but not everything she wanted. All of this occurred long before she was ready to take that gigantic leap! Thus, the intended "plan" of searching for and creating the ideal job with her coach, which was the original agenda, was not to be. This meant both Minerva and her coach, Floreen, had to be willing to be flexible in terms of the coaching. Rather than *creating* the ideal job, it became more important to focus on the immediate need of whether the ideal had emerged on its own. Ultimately, the job turned out to not be the ideal Minerva was looking for, but she didn't know that until after three interviews with the company! Minerva and Floreen purposely focused on going through the steps to ensure the job was right, versus making assumptions that it had to be the ideal. This paid off in the end because in the last interview Minerva saw danger signs that she may not have seen if she had gone into the process blindly. Plus, she now has valuable experience to apply to her next interview process. The following is a small portion of the email coaching that transpired between Minerva and her coach, which helped her prepare for one of her interviews. It starts out with Minerva's response to an assignment that Floreen gave her in the last email—"review the job description from a new perspective." Keep in mind that each interaction below (PBC, COACH) is a separate email.

PBC/MINERVA: "Based on your email, I reviewed the new job description that was shared with me with a more 'objective' eye—looking at the marketing versus editorial weights. I also shared the document with my husband. His insights were especially helpful. He pointed out that the description clearly represented a 'marketing' job, with little—proportion wise—emphasis on editing tasks. He noted, though, that I've done all of the tasks listed and, in environments other than my current job situation, have always seemed to like doing the work. What are your thoughts on whether the most recent bad job experience has made me skittish about tasks I've previously enjoyed?"

COACH/FLOREEN: "Glad to hear you are working on your assignments !:-) Your question is a very good one. Ask it of yourself. What is your answer? Also ask yourself what it is you would need out of the next role in order to not feel that way again? Please let me know your answers."

PBC/MINERVA: "Floreen, how much of my distilling down only to the tasks I enjoy most is appropriate to an 'annual career checkup,' and how much is me distancing myself from everything involved with the past 2 ½ years?" (In her toxic workplace.)

COACH/FLOREEN: "Another good question. Depending on your answers to the questions to the previous email, ask yourself if you really want a change in what you do (i.e., editing vs. marketing), or will a positive change in environment do the trick? Based on what you've told me, you have enjoyed marketing in the past. You are not doing it now and you dislike your current role [sales]. You are also not in an environment that feeds your spirit or your soul. This may go back to your list of 'non-negotiables.' [A previous assignment] Is editing on that list? Or is it bigger than that? Listen to your intuition—what is it saying? Trust it."

PBC/MINERVA: "Uh-oh! I need a sidetrack from the last email. The hiring manager and the prospective company have unexpectedly escalated the hiring process! The first time we met (the information-only interview I requested to find out more about this company), I asked whether we could meet again for me to gather more information—about the company, its benefits, culture, community, etc. We agreed that that would be the nature of our next meeting and I wasn't expecting a formal 'interview.' She sent me an agenda for the day, which includes meeting with her, her boss, and the HR rep, but she said she really wants the company president/publisher to meet me, and so she set up an appointment with him as well. I don't understand why I would need to meet with him during an 'information gathering interview' and, as a result, feel this process is being ratcheted up in inten-sity and so is my anxiety level. I could use your guidance in two specific ways: (1) tactics to level my anxiety with this mushrooming beyond my comfort level and (2) some thoughts as to possible questions I can pose to the president/publisher during my interview."

COACH/FLOREEN: "I can tell you are stressed about this and need an answer quickly so I'll get right to the point. Consider the following coaching questions: First, are you willing to meet with all of these people so quickly? If so, then I will include some sample questions for you to ask below. If not, what boundaries do you need to set? Give yourself permission to do this now; otherwise you will begin the process of handing over your power to them very early, which is something you said you want to stop doing because it's a pattern for you. In other words, are you agreeing to her schedule to be ac-commodating? In your initial response to the question above, did your immediate response come out of a fear or lack of control over the process? Was it because someone was messing with your 'plan'? Where did it come from? Based on that, is there a conversation that you need to have with the hiring manager? Are there any bounda-ries you need to set with her? Better yet, what questions can you ask of her to find out her intentions so you are not making assumptions about what these meetings are all about (devil's advocate)? Maybe this is her idea of helping you 'information gather.' If so, what do you need? Are you prepared to ask for it? What is the hiring manag-er's timeline? Is she willing to accommodate your needs in the process, even if it tweaks her agenda and timeline? How flexible can you be without compromising your needs?

"Per your request, below are the questions that I would ask today if I were looking at a job in the corporate world (they are, of course, optional for you to ask). Also—think of your current situation and the way senior leaders behaved in regard to your prior boss. What do you want and need to know about this company so you can protect yourself from another occurrence like that? One additional sidenote: *Are there also ways to find out more about the job duties during this part of the interview process? (The ones we were discussing in the email stream previous to this one.)*"

"Questions for Senior Leaders"

1. How would you describe the pace that this organization/division is operating at?

2. What systems are in place that support the pace?

3. What remains a challenge in supporting this pace?

4. What tools and resources are offered to team members/managers that allow them to be successful in this environment?

5. How do you measure whether what you are doing as a leader is working in the organization?

6. What is your approach in setting expectations and direction from the top down?

7. How do you as a leader balance the importance of watching the numbers versus leading the people?

8. How do you address situations where people have the skills needed but don't match your culture/values? (This is for you to assess how they do with diversity and given the ultra-conservative nature of the organization.)

9. What things do you do to model and encourage balance among your staff?"

"Pay attention to the words they use when answering—positive versus negative language—look for clues in their body language and evaluate pauses for processing versus BS :-). Use your intuition in assessing each person's answers.

"Hope this helps! You will get through this !:-)"

PBC/MINERVA: "Thanks, coach! This gives me what I need to prepare. I'll keep you posted."

In this email coaching conversation sample, you may have noticed that some questions have more context than in face-to-face conversations. This is to avoid the obvious potential for misinterpretation and miscommunication. You may also have noticed that some emails have more questions than others, and there is higher frequency of closed questions used (than in verbal conversations) for clarification purposes. Keep in mind that in email coaching the PBC can take time to process and reflect on each question and idea.

Did you notice that when Floreen offered suggestions, it was clear that Minerva did not have to use them (it was not about Floreen's solutions)? For instance, the suggested questions offered for interviewing senior leaders were given to Minerva to generate thought and give her a starting point to formulate her own questions for the interview.

One final note is that, just as in face-to-face coaching, this email coaching series diverged off-topic when a different yet pressing coaching need arose. Notice how the coach went with the flow and yet still found a way to make connections to the previous email topic and *refine* (CLEAR) the interaction. If Floreen (coach) had not been able to tie in the previous topic, she would have come back to it after the "emergency" was over to see whether Minerva wanted to pick up where they left off. Another lesson we can learn from this sample is that sometimes when the topic diverges, it is okay to drop the current "agenda' in favor of the new topic, if it is productive and worthwhile in moving the PBC forward toward her goal. In this case, it was.

What techniques can *you* identify as effective in this interaction? How can you use email coaching as an effective tool in your own coaching? What CLEAR coaching skills did you see in this interaction? What stages from the InDiCom model did you identify?

In email coaching, several emails may constitute an entire coaching conversation. Thus, the InDiCom model stage could take more time to complete. This may require you to be more deliberate in moving through each stage.

Coaching Moment

Current Reality: Where did the stages of the coaching model occur in each of the conversations? What skills or elements stood out to you that you want to try in your own coaching?

Ideal State: What does being a skillful coach look/feel like for you?

Action Plan: If you haven't made the mental shift to coach yet, what is holding you back? How can you work to make the shift a reality? If you have made the shift, how will you approach coaching differently in the future? What elements of Coaching for Commitment are you determined to master?

Chapter Summary

There are several sample coaching conversations in this chapter, and each one deals with a specific situation or issue. In some cases the PBC is approaching the coach to talk (PBC's *why*) and in other cases it's the coach approaching the PBC (coach's why). The coach is sometimes a peer, sometimes a manager. Each example uses the InDiCom coaching model and the CLEAR coaching skills and assumes a trust relationship between the PBC and the coach.

CHAPTER 9

Creating a Coaching for Commitment Culture

"If we value independence, if we are disturbed by the growing conformity of knowledge, of values, of attitudes, which our present system induces, then we may wish to set up conditions of learning which make for uniqueness, for self-direction, and for self-initiated learning."

—Carl Rogers

I F THE CULTURE you work in already embraces coaching, congratulations, you are strides ahead of others. Whether you are starting from scratch or building on an existing coaching culture, because coaching is all about improving and maintaining sustained superior performance, we encourage you to look for small and large ways to create or enhance your coaching culture.

The goals relevant to today's coaching culture are as much about conducting coaching as they are about managers being challenged with creating ideal conditions for coaching to occur and creating a self-sustaining environment of coaching. This chapter addresses these goals and challenges and provides a plan for creating a Coaching for Commitment Culture on your team, in your organization or corporation.

Everyone has opportunities to coach, and the overall performance of the organization or entity is improved when more and more people assume that responsibility. Coaching is not a function limited to people with *assigned* leadership or management roles. The most successful coaching cultures thrive because coaching happens up, down, and sideways—and it happens continuously.

Take for instance a high-performing team. On such a team it is typical to find that leadership roles shift easily from one member to another. Each time members take the initiative to help their teammates learn, solve problems, improve, set goals, excel, or plan performance strategies, they act as leaders. The more teams become self-sufficient and self-managed, the more obvious it becomes that leadership is a *shared* responsibility. In high-performing teams, the leadership is usually exercised by anyone who can help the team perform at its fullest potential—that is, *anyone can be a leader*. The practical meaning of this is that members of the best teams are always helping the team and individuals on the team to learn and solve problems—that is, *they coach*. The more coaching happens in a team setting, the more high-performing the team becomes. The process is reciprocal. Just imagine an entire organization in which the majority of teams are high performing. . . . Now *there's* a value proposition for coaching!

What Does a Coaching for Commitment Culture Look Like?

Every organization, regardless of industry or size, can benefit from *being* a coaching culture. Typically, the most effective Coaching for Commitment Cultures start from the top down, where executives participate in coaching others, have coaches themselves, buy in to the coaching culture, and, above all, model coaching behaviors to their direct reports, who in turn do so with others. If you think the top-down approach to creating a Coaching for Commitment Culture is not possible in your organization (for whatever reason) or it's outside your scope of influence, *please* do not abandon the idea altogether! It is still possible to bring coaching into your organization and to create a coaching culture, even if the "culture" is limited to your own team. Coaching for Commitment *can* happen at any and all levels. The scope of a Coaching for Commitment Culture can be as small as a two-person team or as large as an entire organization.

A Coaching for Commitment Culture is one in which:

- Coaching for Commitment is considered an organizational or team value and is represented in the mission and vision statements.
- Everyone understands what Coaching for Commitment is.
- Coaching for Commitment is a common language shared by everyone.
- Coaching for Commitment occurs at every level of the organization.
- Coaching for Commitment behaviors are modeled consistently.
- Coaching is used to encourage empowerment and innovation.
- Coaching initiatives and outcomes are measured in the organization's or team's score card.
- Coaching objectives are included in managers' or teams' objectives.
- Individual 360-degree feedback for leaders and managers (one and two-down) is used to evaluate the success of coaching.
- Team-member surveys include questions around the effectiveness and use of coaching.
- Regular PBC-driven, one-on-ones are part of the culture.

- Peer-to-peer coaching networks exist.
- Bottom-line impacts are seen as a result of Coaching for Commitment.
- Coaching is based on positive intent and is positively regarded.
- Coaching works!

Create a Value Proposition for Coaching

A value proposition answers the question of why you are doing something. What are the benefits? What makes it worth your time and effort?

So, why coach? Successful coaching achieves the long-term result of new and renewed commitment to superior performance, sustained growth, and continuous improvement while maintaining positive relationships, which ultimately creates high-performing individuals and teams, and an increase in your bottom line.

A Coaching for Commitment Culture takes hold and works to promote positive work habits, positive communication, and creativity among *all* team members, all of the time. It is an environment that speaks to respecting individual inventiveness, fostering team cohesiveness, and providing people with the tools and resources they need to do their jobs to the best of their ability. Trust is implicit and individualization has far-reaching effects to the group dynamic. This kind of environment is contagious and is one in which people want to show up and do their best every day because they are heard, understood, and know how they contribute to the overall value and mission of the organization. It can make you an employer of choice!

To create your own value proposition for coaching, answer the following questions:

- What's in it for everyone involved?
- What is our purpose in embracing coaching and creating a Coaching for Commitment Culture?

- What are we trying to achieve by creating a Coaching for Commitment Culture?

- How will creating a Coaching for Commitment Culture change things?

- What is the power of coaching?

- What outcomes will be achieved by creating a Coaching for Commitment Culture?

- Once you have your insight as to the benefits and purpose of coaching, you can condense your answers into short, concise value proposition statements, such as the samples provided here.

Value Proposition Samples

- "Coaching creates a culture of honest and direct two-way communication, high performance, and positive ownership of results."

- "Coaching will provide us autonomy within our jobs, which keeps us engaged and motivated."

- "Coaching is a way of allowing you to be an active participant in your work life."

- "When we coach each other, we all reap the benefits of success!"

How to Create a Coaching for Commitment Culture

To create a Coaching for Commitment Culture, use the InDiCom coaching model as a guide: get people *involved, discover* how coaching is currently used, and *commit* to using a common coaching language.

The InDiCom Coaching Culture Guide, shown in Exhibit 9.1, is a useful tool for organizing your ideas and creating a plan. By working your way through the questions outlined in the guide, you can create an action plan for creating your coaching culture. Answer the questions individually, in groups, or as a team. Get people involved and garner buy-in along the way. Changing a culture takes sustained effort and commitment toward a common goal. This guide was designed to make you think about what you can do to have lasting effects. Don't rush through it as if it were just a checklist. Really think about how you will go about implementing your action plan for creating a Coaching for Commitment culture.

Exhibit 9.1. InDiCom Coaching Culture Guide

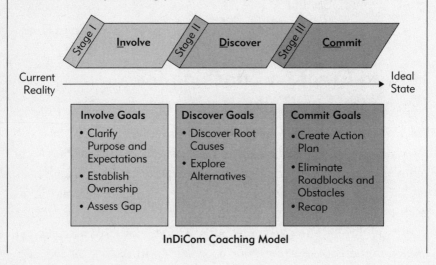

InDiCom Coaching Culture Guide

The stages and goals of the InDiCom coaching model (see below) provide a process for creating your Coaching for Commitment Culture action plan. The guide consists of stage-specific questions. Answer these questions from a perspective that makes them applicable to your world. Although you can complete this guide individually, for best results, complete it with your team and/or stakeholders. Stakeholders are defined as those who are investing in the initiative or anyone (including employees) who has something to gain from its success. Start by creating your value proposition for coaching.

Stage I — **Involve**   Stage II — **Discover**   Stage III — **Commit**

Current Reality ──────────────────────────────────▶ Ideal State

Involve Goals	Discover Goals	Commit Goals
• Clarify Purpose and Expectations • Establish Ownership • Assess Gap	• Discover Root Causes • Explore Alternatives	• Create Action Plan • Eliminate Roadblocks and Obstacles • Recap

InDiCom Coaching Model

Our Value Proposition for Coaching

What's in it for everyone involved?

What is our purpose in embracing coaching and creating a coaching culture?

What are we trying to achieve by creating a Coaching for Commitment culture?

How will creating a Coaching for Commitment culture change things?

What is the power of coaching?

What outcomes will be achieved by creating a Coaching for Commitment culture?

Stage I: Involve
Clarify Purpose & Expectations—Establish Ownership— Assess Gap

Project scope: Check the box that indicates the organizational level you are creating this plan for.

☐ Organization
☐ Region
☐ Division
☐ Department
☐ Team
☐ Other:

Who are the key stakeholders?

How is coaching currently used or portrayed?

What is the current perception of coaching (positive or negative)?

What is the ideal culture we are hoping to create (vision)?

What is the gap between current culture and ideal state?

What are our expectations?

Continued

Stage II: Discover
Discover Root Causes—Explore Alternatives

What has contributed to the current culture?
What does living the ideal culture look like?
What is our shared definition of coaching?
What perceptions (about coaching) need to be validated or dispelled?
What shifts need to occur in order to accommodate a new culture?
What needs to happen in order for us to support our value proposition?
What support do we need? From whom?
If needed, what is our redefined gap?
What research do we need to do?
What do the stakeholders need to know?
What do we need from our stakeholders?

Stage III: Commit
Create Action Plan—Eliminate Roadblocks & Obstacles—Recap

How will we get what we need from our stakeholders?

How do we move forward to reach our goals?

What steps should we include in our action plan (short term & long term)?

How will we begin to close our gap?

How will we create a common coaching language?

How will we dispel current perceptions (if applicable) so coaching is viewed with positive intention?

How will we teach the coaching concepts (model and skills) to others?*

Who will be responsible for what steps?

Who do we need to present our plan to for buy-in?

What challenges will we face (and from whom)?

How can we overcome these challenges?

How will we keep the Coaching for Commitment culture alive?

How will we measure our success (and how often)?

How will we know when we have reached our ideal?

*A *Coaching for Commitment Discussion Guide* is available through Pfeiffer.

Gaining Commitment to a Coaching for Commitment Culture

"I am an idealist with no illusions"

—JFK

As much as we would like to, we do not live in a Utopian world. Creating a Coaching for Commitment Culture is no small undertaking! The fact is that most people do not have a clear understanding of coaching in this form, and many have experienced coaching from a negative perspective. Even the very best leaders and managers on their way to becoming successful coaches ask very tough yet valid questions when trying to address the complexity of shifting to a Coaching for Commitment Culture. We would expect nothing less!

The following FAQs (frequently asked questions) are those we have encountered over the years when helping others to integrate coaching into their cultures. Responses have been crafted to address the challenges you, too, may face in creating your own Coaching for Commitment culture. Learning from lessons of others and being proactive in overcoming resistance is an ongoing step in the process. If you follow the other guidelines provided so far in this chapter, and keep the following questions and answers in mind, gaining commitment to creating a Coaching for Commitment Culture will be easier!

Q: We are taught, and have taught others, that coaching means giving the answer. How do we now change that way of thinking?

A: Creating a Coaching for Commitment culture does not happen overnight. It requires a shift in thinking on the part of everyone involved. Re-educating people about what coaching is and its power can be a good start. Sometimes, the "prove it" to them method works best—start by modeling the way!

Q: How do I find the time to coach when it is faster to give them the answers?

A: Coaching for Commitment does *at first* require a larger investment of time, but the time saved in the end is worth the time invested up-front. Second, it may be faster to give them the answers now, but unless you are planning on working until you are one hundred years old, isn't it time to break the cycle of dependency and foster independence?

Q: People have so many strong opinions about what coaching looks like or is all about, how do you gain consensus?

A: This question creates a lot of angst for many coaches. As easy as it would be to say that one way is best, that is not an effective or realistic answer. You and your organization must develop a shared value proposition and definition of coaching based on shared ideals, principles, and the goals you are trying to achieve, making every effort to place people first in the process. Then build commitment to your coaching culture by working toward making that definition a reality in your world, every day.

Q: If I stop telling them what to do and/or how to do it, won't they lose confidence in me as their leader?

A: Not if you are replacing telling with coaching. If anything, they will begin to understand how much confidence you have in them and they will admire you more for that than any answer you have ever given them!

Q: If I don't continue to come across as tough, they could see a chink in my armor and try to take advantage of me.

A: Yes, they could. And what would be the worst thing that would happen if they did? To be an effective coach you should be authentic. Authenticity is not a synonym for weak.

Q: I get so irritated when team members don't do things the way I think they should, especially when it comes to overtime and taking breaks. I wonder if I will ever get comfortable with asking and not telling?

A: Do you want to get comfortable with it? If your answer is "yes," check your ego at the door and allow them to have answers based on their values, knowledge, experience, and insights. Is there any jealousy lurking within you? How are you doing with setting your *own* work/life balance boundaries? Your values may not be the same as theirs, allow them *theirs*.

Q: How do I know I can trust them?

A: You don't. How does your manager know he or she can trust you? Take a leap of faith. Coaches trust. Be willing and open to truly operate in the *coach role* to see the positive results that come from coaching. If it doesn't work, you have three other roles (*manager, mentor, and instructor*) to choose from.

Q: What if I do this coaching thing and they don't take it/me seriously?

A: What does the PBC or team need to know going into the creation of a coaching culture or coaching conversation so that they see it as a benefit to them and something you're serious about? Coaching requires a shift in thinking that not everyone is always willing or able to make. Are you up to the challenge? If you don't want them to think this is something fluffy, soft, or a flavor of the month, prove it by modeling the way and let them in on the secret of what coaching is all about. Use the *Coaching for Commitment Discussion Guide* (sold separately) to help you.

Q: What do I do when I start coaching on something that I used to give them the answer for and they tell me, "It's your job. Now you want me to do your job, too?"

A: Who taught them it was your job in the first place?

Q: How do we prove to people that coaching is positive?

A: The same way you proved it was negative. Start modeling it from a positive perspective. If you have a "principal's office" in your building where people go "to get coached," start by getting rid of the principal office approach and take your coaching conversations elsewhere.

Q: What if I don't really want to know their answers?

A: Don't ask. You shouldn't ask a question unless you are ready and willing to be open to and hear the answer. In other words, if you can't be egoless, wait until you can be. Until then, use a different role: *manager, mentor,* or *instructor*.

Q: I keep trying to practice my coaching, but they either sit there in silence until I finally give them the answers, or they give me a one-word or standard response. What do I do?

A: They're testing you. Probably unknowingly. They (a) no longer know how to think for themselves, (b) choose the path of least resistance and give the answer they know you want to hear, or (c) wait you out because they know eventually you will give in and answer for them. You taught them they don't have to have the answers because you always do. It is now your job as the coach to teach them differently. Patience and persistence are key. It also wouldn't hurt to explain what you are trying to do, which is to coach.

Q: Our current company culture is not highly conducive to coaching. How do I make a difference?

A: You model the way! Start with your team by sharing what coaching is and show them how to be skillful and effective coaches, by coaching. (You can always use more practice!) Find other departments that have an interest in coaching and join forces. Provide them with copies of this book and its companion materials. Coaching should not be kept a secret. It is a highly successful, powerful tool that, when integrated successfully into a culture, will positively impact the bottom line. You can use the InDiCom Coaching Culture Guide and the *Coaching for Commitment Discussion Guide* (sold separately) to start making a difference.

Q: My organization talks the talk of coaching but doesn't walk the walk. Everyone either knows that it's lip service, or worse, assumes that what we're doing is actually coaching, when it is not. How can I influence this?

A: This is a difficult one to address because many people who believe that they are coaching really are using one of the other roles: manager, mentor, or instructor. Getting people to change their mindsets about what coaching is may not be easy, but it is possible. Similar to the previous answer, start by modeling the way. You can also provide copies of this book to the key individuals you would like to influence. This book was designed to make people rethink how they coach. You could also provide them with copies of the *Coaching Skills Inventory*. The inventory may illustrate to them that their views of coaching are more likely one of the other three roles of *manager, mentor,* or *instructor*. Our coaching questions to you are, what advice would you give someone else if he or she came to you with this question in respect to his or her organization? What *can* you do? What would the ideal look like? And what is the best that you can hope for?

Above all else, the best way to overcome resistance to coaching is to coach! Seek first to understand, and then use coaching to prove that it works.

If you are trying to create a Coaching for Commitment Culture and require additional input to this process, please contact the authors through InsideOut Discovery, Inc., at (719) 761–5226 or (866) 450–45GO(46) or by visiting www.insideoutdiscovery.com. We would be more than happy to help.

Coaching Moment

This coaching moment looks specifically at creating a Coaching for Commitment Culture from the *team* perspective because for most readers that is where they will begin. Those who have higher organizational aspirations for coaching can broaden the scope and take these questions to the appropriate higher level.

Current Reality: What does the current coaching culture look like in your organization? What is the current coaching culture within your team? How would your team members define coaching? What unspoken messages exist about coaching on your team?

Ideal State: What are the benefits to you, each team member, the team as a whole, and even the company, in implementing a coaching culture? What impact would creating a Coaching for Commitment Culture have on your team?

Action Plan: What does your team need to know about Coaching for Commitment and your commitment to it? How can you create a common language of Coaching for Commitment among team members? What coaching questions can you ask of team members to begin creating (or maintaining if one already exists) a coaching culture? What is one thing you can do to help your team members be better coaches to one another? What is one thing you can do to be a better coach to them?

Chapter Summary

A Coaching for Commitment Culture is one in which everyone knows what coaching is, values it, uses it effectively with one another, and includes it as a part of one-on-ones and performance coaching conversations.

To create such a culture:

- Use the InDiCom coaching model as your guide:
- Get people *involved*.

- *Discover* how coaching is currently used.

- *Commit* to using a common coaching language.

Creating a Coaching for Commitment Culture takes concentrated effort and commitment. It is not something that occurs overnight. Gaining commitment requires that you trust people and be authentic in your approach. Concentrated effort means you model the way and find ways to demonstrate the power of coaching to others. Learning to overcome resistance is helpful in creating your Coaching for Commitment culture. One way you can do this is by remaining egoless and using your coaching value proposition to make it a reality.

FINAL NOTE

This book was intended to provide you with a foundation, along with fundamental tools and resources to build conscious competence around the *coach role* and coaching. Having this knowledge alone won't make you a great coach; nor will having the talent and skill. It is what you choose to do with these things that makes the distinction between *wanting* to be known as a great coach and *being* a great coach.

A common thread that ties together all masters in their field is practice. Appendix D (Personal Coaching for Commitment Plan) and Appendix E (Coach Evaluation) will help you to pursue continued coaching excellence.

Because we care about your coaching success, we wish you the best and challenge you to . . .

Care, Commit, and Coach!

Thirty-Five Coaching Questions

What and *how* questions are the most impactful and compelling and allow you to gain the most information. *What* questions diagnose and solve. *How* questions give clarity and are great for determining specific actions. *Why* questions should be limited to avoid placing blame or encountering defensiveness. Throughout *Coaching for Commitment,* there are many great questions and statements that you can use in your coaching. To assist you with your coaching, the following is a quick reference list of thirty-five coaching questions (some repeated from the chapters and some new ones).

Feel free to copy this list and keep it handy when you are coaching. The list is in no particular order.

1. How are things going?
2. How are you going to make that happen?
3. How can you be genuine/authentic in your response?
4. How can you influence this?
5. How do you feel about that?
6. How do you get the best out of people?

7. How do you let them know?

8. How has that gotten in your way?

9. How is that working for you?

10. How is this messing with your values? (Or rephrase the question and name the value.)

11. Tell me about your role model(s)? (Tie into changing behaviors.)

12. Tell me more.

13. What advice would you give someone in your shoes?

14. What are you afraid of?

15. What are you dependent on?

16. What assumptions are you making?

17. What does the ideal look like?

18. What is draining you/your team?

19. What is the best you can hope for?

20. What is the cost of that action/inaction/behavior?

21. What is the first thing you are going to do?

22. What is the worst question I could ask you right now?

23. What makes you say/think that?

24. What one word describes where you are at now? (Ask with Question 25.)

25. What one word describes your ideal?

26. What should you be modeling?

27. What should you be paying attention to?

28. What should your role be?

29. What three words do you want people to use when describing you? (Ask with Question 30.)

30. What do you need to do to live those three words?

31. What would you do if you did know? (Use when PBC responds with "I don't know.")

32. What would you do if there were no rules? (You can negotiate from here.)

33. What would you like to talk about?

34. What would your best friend/someone you admire tell you to do?

35. What is the underlying emotion you are feeling?

B

Twenty Reality Checks

R eality checks (discussed in Chapter 6) are statements of truth or observations made by the coach that are meant to create an ah-ha or shift in the PBC's thinking or to reveal something that, although not obvious to the PBC, is plainly apparent to the coach or others. Reality checks can sometimes be stated as rhetorical questions. Certain topics come up more than others. The following is a common list of twenty reality checks that you can use in your coaching conversations:

1. You keep telling me that you trust your employees, but your micromanagement says you don't.

2. You are so competitive that you're even competing with your wife on vacation!

3. Your employees are so dependent on your approval, you're paralyzing them.

4. It's not surprising that you don't reward or recognize your employees since you don't require recognition yourself.

5. You are taking on so much responsibility for your team's success, you are actually doing more harm than good.

6. You cannot save everyone from feeling the pain of the upcoming changes. It is better to be honest with them.

7. It appears you are playing the role of mother to your employees more than you are being their leader.

8. You are operating out of fear.

9. It appears you are more concerned with seeking approval than with leading.

10. You are 100 percent accountable for 50 percent of the relationship!

11. You are not responsible for the successes and failures of others.

12. You are operating out of fear versus what you know best.

13. You realize that you are over-controlling this.

14. You consistently over-commit.

15. Just because it is your answer doesn't mean it is the right one. (If needing to make a point that a manager should be allowing employees autonomy.)

16. You realize that, until you change, you will always create this dependency (or situation).

17. There's a difference between reckless and risk taking. Allow risks. Don't be reckless.

18. Do you realize that everything you've said thus far is contrary to what you do?

19. You don't have to be all, TO all.

20. Who taught them it was your job and not theirs?

Twenty Validate and Celebrate Statements

Validate and celebrate, discussed in the CLEAR coaching skills (Chapter 6) as part of the Encourage skill, is essential to getting to the root cause of an issue and recognizing the PBC for their accomplishments. The following is a list of twenty validate and celebrate statements that you can add to your toolbox:

1. You sound _____ [insert feeling]. What is making you _____ [insert same feeling]?

2. I can hear the _____ [insert feeling or emotion] in your voice. Where is it coming from?

3. You're not quite yourself today. Would you like to talk?

4. Thank you for putting in the extra effort! It really helps the team out.

5. You mentioned disappointment [or other feeling/emotion]; tell me what being disappointed [or other feeling/emotion] means to you.

6. I can tell that this is really bothering you.

7. You must feel like you are carrying the weight of the world on your shoulders.

8. Yes, you are right, there are many challenges with _____ [workflow, the process, overload, scheduling, etc.] right now.

9. I can tell you have given this a lot of thought already.

10. That is an idea worth exploring.

11. You should be proud of yourself./I am proud of you!

12. I care about your success./I care about what happens to you.

13. I knew you had it in you!

14. It's perfect enough./Sometimes, it is good enough.

15. I appreciate your sharing this with me; I know it was difficult for you.

16. What a great idea!

17. You are very important to _____ [this team, me, the organization, etc.].

18. I can't imagine what you must be feeling right now.

19. Way to go!

20. Keep up the good work on _____ [be specific]./As long as you keep doing _____ [be specific], you will do just fine!

Your Personal Coaching for Commitment Plan

To become an effective coach, it can be helpful to create an action plan for your own coaching success. Thus, Your Personal Coaching for Commitment Plan is all about you and how you can continue to strive toward excellence in coaching. It is about you, Coaching for Commitment. Please complete the following exercises and questions to create Your Personal Coaching for Commitment Plan.

My Coaching for Commitment Action Plan

Name: Today's Date:

10 = Right on track   1 = Not on track

How would I rate myself on the following:

My use of the Coaching for Commitment   10   9   8   7   6   5   4   3   2   1
approach and skills

My ability to create a Coaching Culture   10   9   8   7   6   5   4   3   2   1

In terms of coaching, I would like to:
• keep doing:

• stop doing:

• start doing:

My current reality versus my ideal is:

How big is my gap?

What would I like to have happen in the next six months regarding my Coaching for Commitment approach and/or skills? In the next year?

I plan to accomplish this by (be specific):

My biggest challenges in implementing my plan will be:

I can overcome these obstacles by:

I will know I have achieved my goals when:

Once you have completed your Personal Coaching for Commitment Plan, review Appendix E for ways to evaluate and assess your ongoing coaching progress.

Evaluating Your Coaching

One ongoing step in mastering *Coaching for Commitment* is to evaluate your coaching. The *Coaching for Commitment* companion training workshop materials cover evaluation and assessment of coaching progress in-depth and allow for coach-to-coach, coach-to-observer, and coach-to-PBC feedback. This appendix provides you with one tool to use in assessing your own coaching development. A similar form is contained in the companion training workshop materials. You can also use the CSI: Observer to gather feedback on your preferred role and coaching skills gap.

If you would like to find out just how well you are doing at coaching, ask!

The following is a quick tool that can be used either for self-evaluation or it can be given to those you coach in order to help you assess your coaching progress. One reminder: the *coach role* can may be new and different for the PBC may. It is recommended that you not use the following evaluation with the PBC until your PBC understands Coaching for Commitment. Refer back to Chapter 9, Creating a Coaching for Commitment Culture, for more on introducing the topic of coaching or pick up a copy of the Coaching for Commitment Discussion Guide (sold separately).

If you are a coach using this tool as a self-evaluation, you will need to be extremely objective. Think of your coaching session as if you had been a third-party observer and rate yourself accordingly. If you are the observer or the person being coached, assess how the coach performed, not the specific content or outcome of the coaching conversation.

COACH EVALUATION

Observer: Rate the skills of the coach, not the topic of the coaching conversation. Using the scale below, rate the extent to which the coach demonstrated the behavior indicated. Be objective in your evaluation and capture examples where possible

5 = To a Great Extent   3 = Somewhat   1 = Not Really

InDiCom Coaching Model	Rating
Coach was attentive to the needs of the PBC?	5 4 3 2 1
Coach focused on clarifying the purpose?	5 4 3 2 1
Coach kept the ownership of the situation on the PBC?	5 4 3 2 1
Gap was identified?	5 4 3 2 1
Coach allowed autonomy and innovation in generating solutions?	5 4 3 2 1
Coach resisted fixing the problem/situation for the PBC?	5 4 3 2 1
Coach facilitated the PBC's creation of an action plan?	5 4 3 2 1
Coach discussed barriers and obstacles?	5 4 3 2 1
Coach had the PBC provide the recap?	5 4 3 2 1
The conversation felt natural.	5 4 3 2 1

CLEAR Coaching Skills

Challenge: Coach used intuition to stay in tune with the PBC?   5 4 3 2 1

Bonus: Coach presented a *request* or *reality check?* Yes/No

Listen: The coach heard and understood what was being said?   5 4 3 2 1

Encourage: Coach used validate and celebrate statements?   5 4 3 2 1

Ask: Coach asked coaching questions (did not lead or rapid-fire questions)?   5 4 3 2 1

Refine: Coach kept the conversation on track and focused on the PBC's accountabilities?   5 4 3 2 1

Bonus: Coach used *Two-Words* or metaphor? Yes/No

Additional Comments (use back of page, if desired):

How to Read Your Scores

If you are planning to give this evaluation to more than one person, total the scores on each evaluation and then take an average of all of them so that you may easily refer to the following key:

A score of 66 to 75 indicates you are doing an excellent job Coaching for Commitment! Keep up the great work and come back to the book to brush up once in a while.

A score of 56 to 65 indicates that you are far above average in your coaching. You can still benefit from more practice. Keep this book close by as a reference guide.

A score of 46 to 55 indicates that you are doing an average job coaching. There is still work to be done! Lots of practice and refreshing yourself on Chapters 5, 6, and 7 will benefit you greatly. Find a coaching buddy—someone who will read this book, help you apply the model and skills, and practice with you. Redo your assessments every two or three months or until you see marked improvement in your scores.

A score of 36 to 45 indicates that, although you are likely trying your best, you are struggling with Coaching for Commitment. Don't give up! Start by re-reading Chapters 2, 5, 6, 7, and 8, as well as any others that reflect where you believe you are lacking in your skills or delivery. Also revisit Appendix D (Your Personal Coaching for Commitment Plan) and find yourself a coaching buddy—someone who will read this book, help you apply the model and skills, and practice with you. Search yourself to see whether this is a method you can truly embrace. If so, ask your team or peers to help you with the skills you are trying to master. Remember that being *egoless* is the key to great coaching! Redo these assessments every month until you see marked improvement in your scores. Move to every three months after that until your scores are consistently above 56.

A score of 35 or below indicates that you may need more than just practice and continued reading, although these are a great start. Ask yourself whether you are really ready to be a coach and are committed to being the best one you can be. If your answer is yes, then do everything you can to follow through with that commitment. Create an action plan that outlines how you can move forward to your goal of Coaching for Commitment. Within that plan, create specific and measurable goals and timeframes. Hold yourself to them and, if you are truly serious, enlist the ongoing help of another coaching professional (possibly an external executive coach) or your HR manager. Find a buddy who will read this book, help you apply the model and skills, and practice with you. Ask the person to evaluate you using this tool every time you practice until you show marked improvement. Continue using the tools from Coaching for Commitment and push yourself by finding "What's in it for you."

It is rare, but some people are truly not cut out for coaching. Others just don't believe in it. Whether you decide to master the art of coaching or not is up to you. Whatever you decide to do, in whatever role you play, give it your best.

REFERENCES

Anderson, M. (2001, November). *Executive briefing: Case study on the return on investment of executive coaching*. Des Moines, IA: MetrixGlobal, LLC.

Carver, R.P., Johnson, R.L., & Friedman, H.L. (1970). *Factor analysis of the ability to comprehend time-compressed speech*. (Final report for the National Institute for Health). Washington, DC: American Institute for Research.

HighGain, Inc. (2000, June). *Sssh! Listen up!: How to bring the critical skill of listening into your business*. Sebastopol, CA: Author.

Kinlaw, D. (1991). *Developing superior work teams*. San Francisco, CA: Pfeiffer.

Kinlaw, D. (1993). *Coaching for commitment: Interpersonal strategies for obtaining superior performance from individuals and teams*. San Francisco, CA: Pfeiffer.

Kinlaw, D. (1999). *Coaching for commitment: Interpersonal strategies for obtaining superior performance from individuals and teams* (2nd ed.). San Francisco, CA: Pfeiffer.

Leonard, T. (2002). *Comparison chart: Conventional therapy v. personal coaching*. Coachville.com.

McGraw, P.C. (1999). *Life strategies: Doing what works, doing what matters*. New York: Hyperion Press.

Merriam-Webster Online Dictionary. (2005). Definition of commitment. Available: www.Merriam-Webster.com.

Right Management Consultants. (2004a, July 13). *Average ROI on coaching measured at nearly six, according to a survey of 100 senior executives released by Right Management Consultants* (press release).

Right Management Consultants. (2004b). *The organizational payoff from leadership coaching.* Philadelphia, PA: Author.

The late Dennis C. Kinlaw was the original author of *Coaching for Commitment*. Thanks to Kinlaw and his creation, Dr. Amy Zehnder and Cindy Coe are now able to continue his legacy.

Coe and Zehnder share a passion for life and coaching! Because of this passion, both of these successful businesswomen and executive coaches agreed to co-author this third edition of *Coaching for Commitment*.

The two naturalized Coloradans share one philosophy: "If you believe in people and they believe in themselves, you can bring out their best." That is what coaching is all about. Coaching has more power to impact your bottom line than any other method.

Cindy Coe, an entrepreneur, author, and former Fortune 50 financial services company learning and development manager, is the president of InsideOut Discovery, Inc. (IOD), a Colorado-based coaching and consulting practice that specializes in executive coaching. Serving clients both nationally and internationally, Cindy is a self-dubbed "Possibility Coach." She has spent her career operating as a strategic partner and developing people by applying the principles of coaching to her work and everyday conversations.

Whether it is onstage, online, on the phone, one-on-one, or in the classroom, Cindy's coaching expertise shines through and leaves people feeling motivated and energized! Cindy is a dynamic and enthusiastic presenter and natural facilitator who believes in engaging her audience with thought-provoking coaching questions and involving them with interactive experiences. Just her presence increases people's energy level and enthusiasm, because she makes it all about them!

In addition to executive coaching, Cindy provides a variety of services to organizations in fields such as financial services, education, healthcare, manufacturing, small business, and non-profit. Her service offerings include coaching, coach training, train-the-trainer, facilitated team building, customer service training, instructional design, and keynotes.

Cindy brings almost twenty years of combined talent and experience to the table. She holds a bachelor of fine arts degree in journalism/communications, a certificate in secondary education, and is a graduate from Corporate Coach University International's Advanced Corporate Coaching Program™ (ACCP). Cindy is a member of the International Coach Federation (ICF) and Coachville.

Amy Zehnder, Ph.D., PCC, maximizer coach, and vice president of InsideOut Discovery, Inc., is an entrepreneur, author, and vice president of learning and development for a Fortune 50 financial services company. She is a recognized expert at managing learning and development, talent management, organization development, and HR functions in large, fast-paced organizations. Amy is a highly respected and experienced executive coach. She is a "Maximizer Coach" who focuses on maximizing people's potential.

Amy has been recognized repeatedly for her strategic vision and for adding value to leadership and management programs. She has worked with hundreds of leaders to achieve exceptional results by improving their leadership effectiveness and tying personal initiatives to business objectives. Amy is a phenomenal speaker and facilitator, as well as a charismatic and engaging presenter.

Amy's twenty years of experience shines through in everything she does. She is a graduate of Corporate Coach University International's Advanced Corporate Coaching Program™ (ACCP) and has her Professional Certified Coach (PCC) certification from the International Coach Federation (ICF). Amy is an experienced project manager, statistician, OD professional, human resources manager, and college instructor. She received her doctorate in industrial and organizational psychology and enjoys creating large organizational development programs from scratch.

Cindy Coe and Amy Zehnder can both be reached through the InsideOut Discovery, Inc., website: www.insideoutdiscovery.com, or by calling either (719) 761-5226 or (866) 450–45GO (46)!

The late **Dennis C. Kinlaw, Ed.D**, received his doctorate in adult education from George Washington University. He had master's degrees from Wesley Theological Seminary and Garrett Theological Seminary and a bachelor of science degree from Florida Southern College. He taught graduate courses for American University, George Washington University, and Virginia Commonwealth University in management theory and practice, human behavior, group dynamics, interpersonal communication, organizational behavior, learning theory, human resource development, program planning and evaluation, and counseling of adults.

Dennis was a consultant to organizations and conducted management training programs. His clients included The Aerospace Corporation, Bell Atlantic Corporation, the Chesapeake and Potomac Telephone Company, Livermore National Laboratory, Louisville Bank for Cooperatives, NASA Goddard Space Flight Center, NASA Headquarters, NASA Kennedy Space Center, NASA Langley Research Center, the National Institutes of Health, the Health Care Finance Administration, and USBI Rocket Booster Corporation.

He was the author of numerous articles in management and training journals; instruments and monographs published by Development Products and Commonwealth Training Associates

Publications; the books *Listening and Communicating Skills: A Facilitator's Package* (Pfeiffer) and *Developing Superior Work Teams* (Pfeiffer); and the first and second editions of *Coaching for Commitment* and the accompanying trainer's package.

Dennis also served as a chaplain in the U.S. Navy, instructor at Virginia Commonwealth University, and president of Commonwealth Training Associates and Developmental Products, Inc.

What will you find on pfeiffer.com?

- The best in workplace performance solutions for training and HR professionals

- Downloadable training tools, exercises, and content

- Web-exclusive offers

- Training tips, articles, and news

- Seamless on-line ordering

- Author guidelines, information on becoming a Pfeiffer Affiliate, and much more

Discover more at www.pfeiffer.com